EMPOWERING STORIES TO ACTIVATE THE DIVINE F̶ ̶ ̶ ̶ ̶ ̶'N

turn point

VOLUME 2

FEATURED AUTHORS

DR. SUE BOARDMAN ✦ BRIETTA LEADER ✦ MARIA A. RODRIGUEZ
DR. MICHELLE TEN KLOOSTER ✦ LEEANN WEHR

Plus Essays from 10 Feminine Leaders ✦ *Compiled by Astara Jane Ashley*

FLOWER *of* LIFE PRESS

Praise

"Could it be that Patti Zachery thrived into the Butterfly while she was writing her chapter, 'From the Caterpillar to the Butterfly'? Isn't that what we all long for? Despite the stuckness of her environment, Patti vulnerably shares her experiences, stages of development, deep insights, and uplifting choices. While doing that, she invites us to review ourselves. She calls with clarity: Please do not waste your time on changing an outdated system. Instead, she ushers us into a new paradigm. Patti is a leader who has—spot on and embodied—come alive. She is one of the people that the world needs now to shift into excitement and wholeness."

—**Annelies Weijschedé,** Amsterdam, initiator of the Mad Hatter Summit 2023 in the Netherlands with a mission for #MentalWhealthRising and #EmergentLiving

"I believe this beautiful embodied practice that Brietta Leader invites us into is much needed in a world that struggles to stay connected in a holistic sense. We appear to be more connected than ever before, but have lost a true connection to Self, to the deeper mystery and wildness of our souls. As a student of Brietta's for over 20 years, I have danced, journeyed, healed, found my power, cried, transformed and found a vehicle to understand and express my unique experience of life. Her work is a gift to the world."

—**Titina van Hoorn,** Shamanic energy medicine practitioner, coach and artist, www.titinavanhoorn.com

"In the book, *Turning Point,* Maria Rodriguez's chapter, 'From Near Death, We Rise Up!' had me engaged in a full body way from the first sentence. It brought me back to the early days of living through a pandemic and the scary and hopeless feelings we all endured. Through the vulnerable sharing of her own experience of turning to faith when surrounded by darkness, Ms. Rodriguez demonstrates the transforming power that can come from remaining open. While the story told is miraculous in its own light, the wise lessons that run throughout about the healing capacity of the collective and trusting one's intuition, leave a lasting mark."

—**Mindy Marx,** LCSW

"In *Turning Point,* the chapter 'Divine Destiny…the gift of breast cancer' by LeeAnn Wehr moves with honesty from fear into action. The chapter is an open-hearted life review of transitions, stirring us with a shift from finding self-love into generosity for others who are suffering and in pain. With a strong message of self-empowerment, LeeAnn offers care and love to others through the ancient wisdom of her life-force energy work. With grace and passion, she offers us both a path of preparation and liberation. This wonderful story helps all of us face the truth of the precarious nature of our lives. It teaches us to grasp the beauty of our precious human lives and to embrace how we may be of service to others. I recommend this excellent expose to anyone who wishes to find joy and peace."

—**Sally Connelly,** MBA, CH, MHNFM

"In 'A Trillion Lifetimes,' BrahmanKyrie takes us down an immensely personal account of being deeply captured in the throes of addiction—when an exhausted voice, for the first time, pleadingly prays aloud for a completely different reality. She leads us through the beauty and rawness of fully facing her traumatic past and shows proof of the life-transforming power that's unleashed when we forgive the seemingly unforgivable, and surrender to a higher power to guide us to a life enriched with divine grace. BrahmanKyrie shares a hopeful map for those looking to move from a life consumed by pain and trauma to one of service, devotion, and ultimate healing."

—**Rox Ashtari,** M.A.

"With love and transparency, Star Thomas-Wyse' chapter in *Turning Point* has gifted us with a roadmap for some of life's most potent transformational moments. Star's chapter traces the outlines of what is to come for many of us, and what is familiar for those who've been through it. I felt my heart open as I walked the road with her, witnessing the rites of passage that appear as our parents and ourselves age. Her words made it safer to contemplate these moments of trial, and believe it is possible to do so with the grace of self-awareness, self-forgiveness, and self-acceptance. True medicine for one and all!"

—**Dr. Rima Bonario,** author of *The Seven Queendoms, A SoulMap for Embodying Sacred Feminine Sovereignty*

"Laura Sullivan's chapter, 'My Cosmic Antenna' will transform your view of your wondrous hair and open the way to a new and enlivened relationship between your hair and the energies of life around you. Laura Sullivan's astonishing story is one seldom told and yet often suffered in silent endurance by women in this culture. Filled with perspective-changing knowledge and essential life practices, it should be read by every young woman beginning life's journey. Wonderful writing. An incredible story."

—**Christiann Howard,** author of *Secrets of Aboriginal Awakening*

"Betz McKeown has stepped out on a cliff to offer us a chapter, 'Unmasked: Becoming the Crown'd Crone'—that is a must-read. There are times in our lives when the truth lies hidden, or parts of ourselves have been abandoned and misconstrued. Betz speaks to this in a profoundly deep and personal way that opens the doorway to address what so many of us have felt inside of ourselves without having a diagnosis. I was riveted to every word she shared and my heart has become more compassionate from reading her story."

—**Diana DuBrow,** Founder, Emerald Temple Holy Anointing Oils;
Co-Founder, Rosa Mystica Mystery School

"Mother...tenacious caregiver...theologue...author...teacher...healing chef... Earth partner...artist...good-trouble maker...friend...dreamer of visions... Matriarch! In this sometimes reflection, some places autobiography, mostly epic poem, in *Creating A Map of Reality!,* Dr. Sue Boardman shares her fears, insights, wonder, and surprise at the turning points she has experienced in her own life, and the ways she has learned to understand, nurture, and grow with them. In her sharing, the turns become pirouettes in a spiritual life-dance! (And this reader senses she is only getting started!)"

—**Marilyn Washburn,** MD, PhD, MPH, FAAFP, FACPM

"In *Turning Point: Empowering Stories to Activate the Divine Feminine Within,* Cindy Fielding-Smith offers an insightful and eloquent reflection of the wonders of synchronicity and heart-knowing of the Divine Feminine within. Her chapter, 'This Little Light of Mine' beautifully reflects the wounds of so many of us. I felt the medicine in her words around the 'need' to dim her (my) light as a young child in order to be less of something to those around her (me). This is a powerful truth that I have been rediscovering in my own life and guiding others to reclaim as well. Through her words and wisdom, Cindy calls us back to remember that light—that divine feminine wisdom within and inspires us to embody that light in this life."

—**Elsa Alegria Perez Dean,** Priestess, Ceremonialist & Transformational Guide, Founder of the Radiant Heart Sanctuary and Intuitive Wisdom for Body & Soul, Author of *Reclaiming My Birthright to Sovereign Power and Joy*

"*Oh, Wow!* is what I said to myself at the finish of Caryl Anne Engel's 'The Party's Over: Welcome Back to Earth School.' In this chapter, Caryl presents an adolescent scenario with vivid detail, with characters including her high school crush, whose lips—'the color of salmon'—she longs to kiss. Such enticing storytelling is uniquely juxtaposed with the overlay of heavenly conversations with her angels, who let her select which family she'll be born into...but not the why of the life lessons she'll encounter in on Earth. I must learn what happens with the characters and situations presaged with the angels, and whether she ever gets to kiss that cute dude, Paul, from her high school musical."

—**Holly Galgano,** Deacon, Episcopal Church, Rye, New York

"LaurenRose EveningSong writes from her artist's heart—poetry & prose, rhythm & rhyme—revealing her evolving awareness of her soul's need to thrive. She courageously invites us to walk with her through her light and her dark; inspiring us to never give up and to be curious about what comes next."

—**Rabbi Dr. Radonsky,** Ph.D, Founder of Watering the Tree Outside the Fence Foundation and the Society of TheVav

"Grab a cuppa tea—and sit down for the delightful ride into the realms of magical storytelling. In her chapter, 'If I Do Not Speak, I Cannot Hear My Voice,' Sarah Devereux paints the picture of how our lives are filled with moments of incredible beauty, deep grief, joy, humor and pain. Take the ride with her and see through her unique eyes to feel the depth of our very human lives—you will find yourself within her words, and roller coaster ride through the snap shots that make up our lives. Sarah is a rare and powerful storyteller."

—**Elayne Kalila Doughty,** MA, MFT, Ordained Priestess, Psychotherapist, Founder, Focalizer & Dean, Priestess Presence Temple + School of the Sacred Arts

"Reading Michele Leeper's chapter, 'The Divine Wild Mother: Becoming Sanctuary' is like pulling up a comfy chair in your best girlfriend's kitchen and receiving a piping hot plate of nourishing soul food. Deliciously wild and raw, she invites you into a juicy story sprinkled with generous helpings of humor and heart that ignites the feminine fire within. Worth savoring!"

—**Pi Venus Winslow,** Transformational Life Coach, Author of *Mother Medusa—Weaving Myth, Ritual, and Magic into Healing from a Narcissistic Upbringing.*

"*Turning Point: Empowering Stories to Activate the Divine Feminine Within - Volume 2* will sweep you up and carry you away, not to somewhere foreign or otherworldly, but into your truest self. The chapter, 'The Body Under the Floor: Resurrecting My Lost, Feminine Essence,' by Dr. Michelle Ten Klooster, is nothing short of a mystery school in nine pages. With goosebumps across my entire body, I hung onto every word following the threads of the deep feminine wisdom she presented. Michelle's vulnerability in sharing her death and resurrection story is a must-read for all women seeking to return to their wholeness. I can't wait to share it far and wide!"

—**Dr. Rima Bonario,** Author of *The Seven Queendoms: A SoulMap for Embodying Sacred Feminine Sovereignty*

FLOWER *of* LIFE PRESS

Turning Point: Empowering Stories to Activate the Divine Feminine Within
Volume 2

Copyright © 2023 Flower of Life Press, LLC

Flower of Life Press
Hadlyme, CT.

To contact the publisher, visit www.floweroflifepress.com

Book cover and interior design by Astara Jane Ashley, www.floweroflifepress.com
Cover art by Sue Boardman, www.sueboardman.com

Library of Congress Control Number: Available Upon Request

ISBN-13: 979-8-9878275-4-3

Printed in the United States of America

Dedication

This book is dedicated to all the Sacred Feminine Voices that have been oppressed and suppressed for eons...

May they be heard, received and honored Always and in All Ways.

To our ancestors who have gone before, we are grateful to you as our way-showers and for your courage in leading the way.

Contents

featured authors

She Takes Her Place Among the Matriarchs

By Dr. Sue Boardman

Dear Reader,

I am a Medicine Painting…an **Intentional Creativity**® Insight painting.

Officially, I am: ***She Takes Her Place Among the Matriarchs.*** Call me Grammy, if you like!

It's my job to help the one holding the brush to use all her awareness on life's very special journey. To explain the journey, I need to introduce you to Fred.

Well, technically Frederick Buechner, who was an author, minister, and theologian. Also, a really nice guy.

He wrote power-full things on a mountaintop in Vermont. Let's start with this one…

The place where we are called is where our greatest joy and the world's deep longing meet.

Part of what Medicine Paintings do is to help people find their way to that place.

It has a lot to do with getting our right and left brains to hold hands and work together to dream and plan the actual steps from here to there.

What you see to your right when you look at me is the dreaming part. All swirly and moving, sprinkled with lots of dots. Dots of intention and prayer.

The honeycomb you see on your left is the plan part. The structure. It takes both dreaming and structure to get where we long to be. (Sue's secret to-do list is hidden under the honeycomb!)

Here's the really cool part, though…it's not just what I—the painting—look like when I'm finished that makes the difference.

Imagine you are painting. You move your hand to make marks. You see them appear on the canvas. You say a name for the mark. *Hope,* perhaps. Or *mattering.*

Like a miracle, all of you is moving toward that place of your deep joy and the world's great longing!

Now, it's not quite that simple, and there's more going on in the image than I can explain right here, but practicing this kind of intention can make a huge difference in our world. That's why it's so exciting!

Lean in, for a minute, please. Do you see the two teardrops below my eye?

Well, our friend, Fred, had something to say about them, too!

That sudden, unexpected flash of tears we get is the surest sign of truth we have.

That's my job!

FREE GIFT

Could you use a Matriarch—a Fiercely Compassionate Grandmother—in YOUR space? A presence to help you live into your intentions???

It's easy! Just click the link to opt-in for a pdf poster of the cover art…Our gift to you! **www.sueboardman.com/turningpointsposter**

Introduction

By Astara Jane Ashley, M.A.
Publisher, Flower of Life Press

Have you ever faced a turning point in your life where you had to make a choice to change? A moment where nothing would ever be the same again?

If you're human, the answer is likely YES.

To me, these moments are initiations, portals of transformation, where sometimes I am shaken to my core and the ground is no longer sturdy. It's a dismantling of who I "think" I am and an evolution into my true essence, fostering spiritual growth.

I believe these turning points are here to help us remember that we are *never* alone. Because when we choose to share our stories, magic happens. Intimacy happens. Permission for living happens. Hope happens.

This is the reason for the book you are now holding in your hands—to empower YOUR inner Divine Feminine by contemplating your own story and turning points. On a quantum level, we are all ONE—just waves in the same ocean. Our individual expressions are so beautiful and unique and artful, and we are here to create, inspire, connect, love, and remember that we *belong* to life.

This is why we share our stories. And because I have invited the authors in this book to bravely share their stories from an authentic and vulnerable place, I thought I better share my latest turning point, too. So here it is:

My dad died last week.

After a long battle with three different kinds of cancer, at age 85, my Dad surrendered to death. I arrived at his bedside 15 minutes too late—he had already taken his last breath while my mom stood nearby. My mom was his beloved wife of 59 years, and his caregiver for many of those years.

A week prior, Dad was on a golf cart, being driven around the land conservation cemetery where his final resting place would be—acreage of meadows filled with stunning wildflowers, emitting a rainbow frequency of colors...it is so peaceful and lush.

We had a green funeral for Dad, and it was incredibly sacred. There was a bagpiper and a Marine Corps salute. My mom was presented the American flag in Dad's honor. They played Taps. Dad was shrouded in an antique quilt that his mother—my grandma—had made. I anointed him with holy oils, and his grandchildren were pallbearers. The kids lowered him into the ground as we took turns shoveling in the dirt and covering him with flowers.

This hands-on experience honoring my dad's death has completely reframed my relationship to life and death. My biggest fear as a kid was the day I would lose him, and here I was, finally experiencing it. It was so painfully heartbreaking yet I was filled with so much gratitude and joy—all at the same time.

I am getting to know grief—slowly. It's unpredictable, this process of the heart. My heart has cracked open and is, strangely, *staying* open—not armoring up as it might on any other normal day. This feels so...vulnerable. Being open-hearted *all the time*...is this even possible?

Right now, I feel the "paradox" of grief. I am ungrounded *and* grounded, tethered *and* untethered, sorrowful *and* joyful, chaotic *and* ordered, loving *and* fearful. I am surrendered to this aliveness, knowing that *not one of us* can escape from this—the loss of a parent.

In the 9 months before Dad's death, I experienced other turning points that initiated me, as well. I was attacked by a dog and my ear was bitten and stitched up, and I had two hospitalizations for kidney stone attacks. I could choose to see these "attacks" as betrayals by life, but I'd rather see them as gifts. I have learned that challenges lead us to grace and to God.

These turning points have led me into a rebirth, like a caterpillar turned to mush in the cocoon, who will soon emerge as a butterfly and take flight into a new life...one that is totally new and exciting—and unknown.

I am now clear that I *belong* to life. The earth is my mother. I am always held and she's not going to let me go flying off into space! Someday I will go home to her.

While riding these waves of grief, I feel deeply held by the Divine. I love my Dad, and he knew it, and he loves me, and I know it. That's pretty darn good! Forgiving myself and others who have betrayed me or hurt me is part of understanding this transformation. Yes, the initiations will continue, because that's what happens in life. But I am discovering that the antidote to suffering is gratitude. I am aware of a deep knowing in my bones that life is *for* me, rather than against me.

I'm trusting this—while I laugh and cry at the same time. (I like to call it "craughing.") Life is a big, cosmic joke—and the Goddess is in on it with me. On either side of the coin is light, love, and beauty, while on the other side is suffering, pain, and fear. We are the coin. We have the capacity to exhibit the entire spectrum of vibration from light to dark. And I am so grateful to take each moment as it comes, with equanimity and valor...as my dad modeled for me.

One of my dad's sayings was, "Janie, you can do anything, as long as you're properly trained." I believe him! I've always jumped into new experiences with both feet and trusted because of his words and his actions. As a kid, I remember watching him sew up his own knee after a cross-country skiing accident—with a needle and thread! He was definitely a Marine.

One thing I do know is that turning points are gifts, meant to poke a hole in our sense of safety and complacency so we can truly see how *life has got us*. And to see that, no matter what, the seed of grace is there, behind the challenge.

Like the yin-yang symbol, the light holds the dark, and the dark holds the light. Change is all we have—it's the only certainty there is. Dad showed me how to embrace change, face my challenges, and say *yes* to life so I can find the light and the love waiting for me.

Thank you, Dad, for showing me how to live, how to love, and how to die with so much authenticity and grace.

The Mystery remains, but whatever it is, it's all LOVE.

CHAPTER 1

Creating a Map of Reality!

By Dr. Sue Boardman

This is my "fractured fairy tale" made new:

Once upon a time, a medium number of years ago, I found myself "wracked and in bondage," not to a person so much—though that had to be dealt with—but to beliefs I had and stories about how life was supposed to be and how powerless I was to change any of that.

Then, one day, I found myself four months pregnant and filing for divorce. The details really don't matter anymore. Go ahead and fill the story in with whatever makes sense to you. I simply could not put a child in the place where I was.

That was a huge turning point. Possibly the first one I chose consciously!

There was no fairy godmother in sight! Well, unless you count the Food Stamp lines and the Student Loan people.

Slowly, I found my way to freedom, ironically led by that little child. Dave.

In the early months of 1985, I began working as a nurse in the operating room of our local hospital.

I'd only been in surgery a few days when an emergency came in, and the surgeons needed more help than they had. I was scrubbed, gowned, gloved, and squeezed into the crowd around the table. "Hold this," a surgeon said, "and don't move."

For the next four hours, I stood, barely breathing, with my hand wrapped around a man's beating heart. I was terrified. My feet fell asleep. My back ached. I needed to use the bathroom. And still I stood, with life in my hand.

Finally, it was over. The patient was wheeled away to recovery and the surgeons scattered to their busy worlds.

I went to wash my hands. Standing at the scrub sink for the second time that day, I was overwhelmed with the certainty that humanity, in all its tremendous complexity and fragility, could not be an accident.

What my hand had learned, through all those long hours of sheltering a beating heart, taught my own heart the truth of a universe created in Love.

A universe that didn't work as well for some of us as it did for others.

Two things were particularly challenging for me in those days of scrubs and masks.

The first was the abundance of very young teen moms on our OR tables for Caesarean sections. Most were under spinal anesthetic, meaning they were awake and universally terrified. None of them were ready to be there!

And all I could do as the circulating nurse was hold their hands and wipe their tears.

One of those girls was 13 and living with significant developmental challenges. Her mother's husband was the father of her child. A girl. I wept with them both.

The second challenge was the frequency with which surgeons told me emphatically that I didn't get paid to think.

Then, just as I was beginning, consciously, to wonder what I wanted to be next, and how I would get there with a very busy 5-year-old, my phone rang.

An elder from the church I grew up in had a favor to ask. The family ministry team was hosting a parenting class. There was a single dad who was interested but reluctant to be the only single parent.

You guessed it—I signed up! That was a turning point, too, though probably not the kind you're imagining!

Enter Dr. H. Stephen Glenn, creator of the ***Developing Capable Young People*** (**DCYP**) course. Steve had some ideas that weren't quite *the way we'd always done it!*

An early ah-ha moment for me was Steve's radically odd notion that *there's no such thing as failure. Only experience to be learned from!* I wanted my son to learn that…and me, too!

Before too long, I was invited to a week of leadership training so that I, too, could teach notions like that one.

We were sitting on the floor in a gymnasium at Rollins College in Florida. About 3,000 of us who cared about kids. Then it happened!

Steve stood up and said that *if a teenaged child had five adults who would listen to them, take them seriously, and not shame them or blame them for their questions, that child was practically immune from ever attempting suicide.*

As you may have guessed, I was on my way back to school. The turning points were picking up speed!

My son was in kindergarten. I was leading **DCYP** groups and going to night school to finish my degree at Eckerd College, where I took a required course called "Life, Learning, and Vocation."

Here's the most important thing I learned…an old Quaker saying:

In order to learn, we must be willing to be changed!

At about the same time, I began to notice scattered inner musings about going to seminary and becoming a pastor.

It scared me so badly that I dropped out of school for 18 months! And then, I went back. My advisor laughed gently with me when I told her my secret. She and my teachers had, apparently, been taking bets on how long it would take me to notice!

It was **not**, in case you're curious, an easy path!

At Columbia Theological Seminary, we began with summer Greek School. I was lost! In fact, I might have quit, except for the fact that I didn't have the money to go home. And then it happened…

Blepo!

The first word I understood…It means *I see* and was familiar from the official names for lots of eye surgeries. There was hope!

It's a good thing there was hope because there was also a whole lot of hard ahead.

Like Hebrew, which was way harder than Greek. Reformed Theology.

An awful nursing job to put groceries on the table. Ordination exams.

Eventually…some very good turning point news!

On a Thursday night in May of 1990, just before my graduation on Sunday, Bill and I got married.

He was a Columbia grad, too, and the wedding resembled a reunion, with a whole lot of church!

Three of our most beloved professors officiated. In his sermon, Dr. Walter Brueggemann spoke of **Concrete Passion and Very Large Hope**…a message which speaks in my heart, still. (It's entirely likely that I understand it even better now than I did then!)

I learned along the way that the stories we tell, the realities we create with our own words, make all the difference. I learned that our stories can be edited and re-formed into tales of freedom rather than bondage.

I also learned along the way that people are not always so fond of the bizarre notion that our stories can be edited! (Perhaps you've noticed that, too!)

A whole lot of that learning happened in a small town in Tennessee, where I was called to serve as solo pastor in my first church.

You can just feel the turning points coming, can't you?

The tiny congregation had struggled for years.

I was not *head of staff*. I **was** the staff. The whole staff. (Well, it wasn't too long before we were blessed with a piano player, that being decidedly **not** among my skills!)

Along with my son, who was 10 by then, I was the church secretary. I was chief in charge of clean bathrooms. When we mowed and baled hay on the acres of front lawn, I was the pest control team, in charge of liberating the field mice who hid in the building during all the ruckus.

I was, as I mentioned, still learning!

I learned that new hymnbooks can be considered blasphemy. (Hint: should you ever find yourself in such a position, only sing the *oldies but goodies* for the first three months!)

I learned that adults also need Steve Glenn's ***five adults who will listen to them, take them seriously, and not shame them or blame them for their questions*** in order to consider options other than suicide. Especially if those adults are victims of domestic violence.

One afternoon I sat with a woman in the church study and listened to her story. Her husband had been battering her for years. After particularly bad injuries, she had gone with her children to a shelter in another Tennessee county.

Her gynecologist—the only female MD in our county—had asked her to speak with me.

She sobbed as she told me she was going back home. And then she said this:

> **If I go back, it might be months before he beats me again. If I don't go back, my three children and I will be hungry every day.**

Yep! Turning point!!!

And the beginning of a shelter and resource site in our county, with a whole lot of help from my dear friends, the Episcopal and Roman Catholic priests, and our neighbors who got it.

There were others who did not get it.

In the three years we were there, the church I served was robbed twice, vandalized three times, and had a bomb threat.

Nothing I ever imagined about serving a church had prepared me for the phone call from the local fire chief one freezing night in February. The church door had been found open when emergency personnel responded to the phoned-in bomb threat. They needed me to come and wait with them while the bomb dogs were summoned from Nashville.

It took a couple of hours. And while we shivered and waited, I prayed.

Blessedly, no bomb was found. No one was injured or killed.

No one was ever arrested.

Good news still happened, as good news does. There and in other places.

More learning happened, too. And I began to claim me. To tell new stories. Stories about things *we* *don't talk about*. The only thing more terrifying than telling those new stories would have been **not** telling them!

Oddly, knees can be pretty terrifying, too. And turning points of their own!

Specifically, six knee surgeries in nine years. A couple of major falls. And a need to learn to tell stories from a magic recliner chair rather than a pulpit.

My doctoral dissertation, focused on pastoral counseling, came in handy. Living the hypnotherapy and guided imagery work helped, too, when it came to coping with the pain.

The stories became books. And tools for coaching clients.

And then an amazing thing happened. A turning point I never saw coming!

I'm guessing you know Susan. Probably by the name **SARK**! She was helping with the book thing and one day, during a private Zoom meeting, she asked if I'd be willing to play a game with her.

And, yes…I said yes!

The *game* Susan had in mind involved Alana Fairchild's **Mother Mary Oracle Cards**. This was **not** something we covered in nursing school or seminary. I listened deep and agreed.

Here's the short version…Susan shuffled the cards and passed them through her hands, 2,000 miles away, until I was ready for her to stop.

6. Our Lady of the Dark Mysteries. Five words: *Our Lady of Fierce Compassion*. Language for what I wanted to live!

And not just language. Images! Divine Feminine images, by Shiloh Sophia McCloud!

A few months later, I, who grew up not being *the artistic kid*, signed on for an adventure called **The Black Madonna Pilgrimage** with Shiloh Sophia and Kayleen Asbo.

Frankly, I was terrified. Not only because the whole paint thing was so new, but because the theological tradition in which I was raised and trained has not, historically, been a fan of images.

Despite my fear and the fact that I was raised primarily in the Southern United States, where *Black* and *Madonna* were among the things **we** didn't talk about, I felt deeply drawn to the space I felt in Her presence. Space for my own interpretations, as I gazed at the richness and depth of the symbols.

My pilgrimage painting became my externalized *Lady of Fierce Compassion*.

Pause, please, for a chorus or two of *I once was lost but now I'm found…was blind but now I see!*

It turned out that I could use all of me for learning!

In the land of Neurolinguistic Programming, we'd say I could use all of my processing patterns.

I knew the Kinesthetic (feelings and motion) well. Auditory/Digital (basically, words) too. But gaining access to the Visual was, indeed, a turning point!

My hands, which once taught me about Creation, wrapped around a stranger's beating heart, were teaching me again…wrapped around paint brushes. I felt like I was holding my own heart—beating in a way I had never noticed before—which felt just as profound as holding another person's beating heart!

All of those things are true.

There are, however, other true things as well.

I have two granddaughters. Mighty mini women growing and learning by leaps and bounds. Full of questions.

And, I seem to have been on this journey much longer than I ever realized.

I feel as though I've discovered parts of me, of my heart, and my deep, deep history, that I never knew before. It's exciting. Especially when my girls paint and share stories with me!

These days, I am honored to be a certified **Intentional Creativity**® **Teacher & Coach** and a **Red Thread Guide.**

It is not an overstatement to say that I am free. I have many, many ways to fashion new stories. To **choose** my understanding of myself and my journey. To heal the old stuff and make way for new.

That's called *Medicine Painting.*

And, even though I know how it works, I just amazed myself with an **Intentional Creativity**® adventure called *Apothecary.*

It started out feeling comforting and familiar. Intention. Lots of fun drips, hither and yon, as I turned the canvas. (I like drips!)

A line. In my case, a dark, jagged one, kind of like a lightning bolt. The line of *unimaginable tragedy.*

Eventually, we got to the part about vessels.

Think *Apothecary*, as in remedies for ailments. Kind of like a pharmacy. (An open-minded one!)

The books appeared first. Books are vessels, too!

Then, after a busy night dreaming, a stock pot. This isn't new to me, for I am a boiler of bones.

The night sky. And my version of a Phoenix rising right out of the stock pot, complete with a bay laurel leaf!

Then, things began to get interesting.

An alabaster jar, which is a sign that my collection of sacred stories and symbols is growing.

The face and the arrow on the stockpot are related to something nicknamed *Filters,* which I was introduced to long ago by a guy named Bill Harris. Familiar, for sure, but, ironically, completely new in the context of the painting!

Frankly, I was feeling a bit anxious about the *Apothecary* painting. There was still something missing.

Yep! A circle, on the stockpot, with six thumbprints.

A six-petal rose. Right there, where my *map of reality* belongs! Utterly by choice!

Tears. Relief. Hope. A whole new world, in many ways.

I thought I was finished. But the painting was not done speaking to me.

The next morning, she announced her name.

Revelation!

Which is a whole lot like a turning point!

So many things make more sense now! A 30x40 inch map of what I feel called to be in this world.

Birthing story-symbols which help me to fashion new inner stories… stories that are empowering and more true…to free myself over and over again and to risk helping others on the road.

With clients only daring to hope that change might actually be possible for them. With folks praying that the 7 o'clock news isn't the only story there is. With rescue dogs. And with grandchildren who have the amazing chance to learn better, stronger stories the first time through!

We are meant to keep learning. And this, for me, is what it looks like to *take my place among the matriarchs*!

Often Kleenex is involved! And, paint!

Note…The "wracked and in bondage" quote with which we began is Anne Lamott quoting Toni Morrison.

A brief bibliography…

Brueggemann, Walter. ***Finally Comes the Poet…daring speech for proclamation***, Fortress Press, 1989.

Buechner, Frederick. ***Whistling in the Dark—an ABC Theologized***, Harper & Row, 1988.

Glenn, H. Stephen & Jane Nelsen. ***Raising Self-Reliant Children In A Self-Indulgent World***. Prima Publishing & Communications, 1989.

Harris, Bill. ***Thresholds of the Mind***. Centerpointe Press, 2003.

DR. SUE BOARDMAN

Sue Boardman says, "I am still learning!"

And, indeed she is. A former R.N., Sue received Master of Divinity and Doctor of Ministry degrees from Columbia Theological Seminary in Decatur, GA. She served the Presbyterian Church (USA) for 25 years as a pastor and pastoral counselor.

Much of Dr. Boardman's work has been with families and couples. She has been a certified leader for the *Developing Capable People* program for more than 30 years and has mastery level training in Ericksonian Hypnotherapy and Neurolinguistic Programming. Her doctoral dissertation was entitled, *Will You "Do" Our Wedding*, a subject which has taken on new meaning in recent years.

Sue is the author of two #1 bestselling books, **Grandmothers Are In Charge of Hope** and **We Gather Together…holiday feasts with the family you have!** Her twice-weekly blog can be found at **www.sueboardman.com** and focuses on meeting the challenges of having 2 granddaughters growing up in this world.

One day in 2017, she set out on an adventure known as *The Black Madonna Pilgrimage* and has learned even more, completing certifications as an **Intentional Creativity® Teacher, Coach, and Red Thread Guide.** Dr. Boardman uses her many filters to help others, privately and in groups, on their paths to the place often described by the late Frederick Buechner as *where their deep gladness and the world's deep hunger meet.*

FREE GIFT

Is there part of you longing to rise up—like a Phoenix—out of the soup pot of this world, now?

The next steps start here **www.sueboardman.com/turningpointsgift**

You might do kind of like Dorothy and click your heels and say:

I'm curious! I'm willing! I'm ready!!!

Your free gift—super tasty tips on real transformation in your world—is waiting for you!

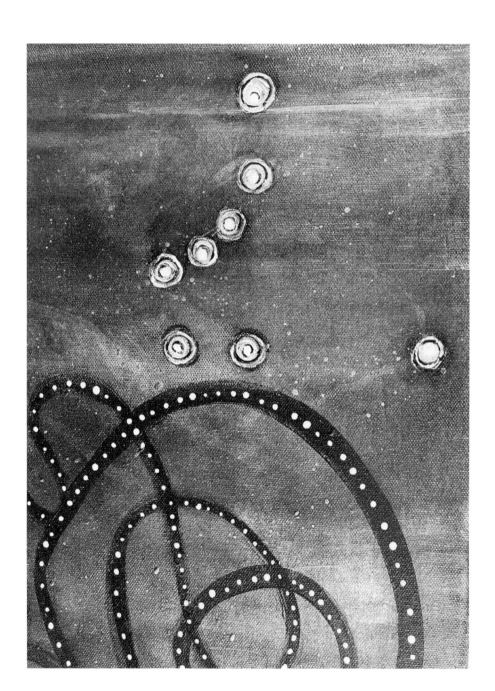

Featured Author

CHAPTER 2

Turning toward Self-Love

By Brietta Leader

Self-love is a vibration that moves through the core of our bodies. Each of us has our own unique way of defining and choosing self-love. Many of us will never question whether we love ourselves. Loving yourself can feel so obvious, yet if you have done personal work, you may find that your habits are not tethered to your worthiness, but to the desire to feel accepted. Or, you may consistently turn toward pleasing others and leaving nothing for yourself.

It can be alarming to realize that self-doubt, unworthiness, or feelings of not being enough are related to our lack of self-love. Our dance with self-love may inspire us to turn inward and hug closer to the path that nourishes us, or, at other times, turn away to stumble, wobble and fall along the way. Some of us can spend years turning away from this inner need to love ourselves and consistently choose a path of struggle. In general, I believe that many of us choose the path of struggle because it is what we are most familiar with or we don't realize there could be other options. The persistent challenges that derail us from the frequency of our own self-love will be the doorway to deeper healing. When we recognize the value of our self-regard or that ability to appreciate our positive aspects—and our negative—and still feel good about ourselves, we can start to identify the inner compass that points us to our pathway to self-love, no matter how many times we have to recalibrate.

My life journey harmonizes the interplay of the wilds of the natural world with the inner wild we discover when we dance. The inner wild that I am talking about cannot be defined. It is something that Mother Nature is the best teacher of, and it is a part of us that is easily lost as our modern lifestyles keep us adapting to screens, ease, and disconnection from life rhythms. Wildness can be an urge, an inner impulse to escape the norm and find the inner edge that makes you feel alive. If we are deprived of our own aliveness, we may feel the self-regard waver and circulate in waves of energy that keep us in a lower frequency. This vibration may feel the safest, and accessing the courage needed to turn toward self-love could feel unreachable.

I have explored pathways of tracking my natural tendencies toward self-love, which have become the key codes for listening to my energetic heart. In this exploration, I discovered layers of being with the practice of self-love that are triggered naturally through the instinctive and intuitive parts of the body, which I share below. The key code to self-love leads us to the realization that there may be many turning points within our dance to understand self-compassion, self-worth, self-regard, intimacy, and love— all of which need as much tending as a living fire. Like a real fire we require fuel to burn brightly, and a relationship with our body's innate wisdom gives us the insight we need. There are several layers within this key of self-love: instinctual, intuitive, contracted, and expanded.

Instinctual self-love

It is the second day on the river, and I am soaked again. This time, it is raining and the perfect temperature to become hypothermic. I have not found my combination of clothing layers to stay comfortable sitting in a raft as we float along the Tatshenshini River that flows from a remote section of British Columbia into Alaska.

My instinctual love for Self was kicking in. My inner drive to survive knew that I needed to speak up and tell the group that I was wet, cold, and starting to shiver. We pulled over and I discovered that I wasn't the only one suffering. One of the group members pulled out the fire pan and, remarkably, found some dry wood for a warm fire. Meanwhile, I was head-first in my huge dry bag digging for a set of warmer clothes. My friend Yvette was there to help me as the tears started to stream down my face. I was losing the dexterity in my wrists and fingers due to the cold and now all of my other gear was getting wet in the rain.

All of this might seem minor on a day trip, but we were on day 2 of a 12-day river trip that continued into the remote wilderness with glaciers, icebergs, and more rain. This moment was a turning point—a reminder to pull it together, get what I needed fast, close my bag, drink some tea, and warm my body by the fire. Instinctual self-love shows up in the moments when our body's will to survive overrides anything else.

This quality of love is connected to our primal body, our first chakra. This energy center is our foundation or roots, making sure we are in a safe environment, our body is nourished, and we have a sense of belonging. You may have similar stories that represent this instinctual self-love, even if you were feeling low. This is why Mother Nature is such a great teacher; she wakes us up to feeling alive. She tests our will to survive and encourages us to increase our strength, so we can walk with confidence and a sense of belonging in any circumstance.

Intuitive self-love

I was several days into my conscious dance practice when I tipped toward self-love. The awareness of my life-force leak became clear as the message, "I am done pleasing others for the sake of feeling accepted" landed in my heart. It was a lightning bolt of clarity and an opportunity to claim my power back. Intuition is such a powerful resource...truly a superpower that everyone has access to. We have all had those moments when we kick ourselves for not listening to the inner voice that knew to wait for the snowstorm to pass or to double-check whether the candle was blown out or the oven turned off.

Our intuition is constantly communicating with us through bodily sensations, impulses, and inner knowing. The best way to expand your intuition is to listen to it and follow through with the hints you receive. Anytime we second guess ourselves, we are sure to pay the consequences. Intuitive self-love maintains the inner state of equilibrium and balance—and works to maintain it.

Naturally, intuitive self-love occurs when you feel injustice and you tip toward standing up for yourself and creating a boundary. In fact, our ability to create boundaries is like filling up our internal bank account with all the funding and resources we need to stay empowered. If you are like me, you have noticed times when you said 'yes' to a job, a volunteer project or favor that your intuition did not line up with and right away you felt the drain of energy and lack of enthusiasm. This is a form of giving your power away. These are the moments you can turn around for yourself as you dance with self-love and say 'no' when your body response is less than desirable.

Intuitive self-love shows up when you plan a nourishing hour, day, or weekend filled with your favorite creative outlets and treatments to refill your energetic cup. Intuition can be exercised like a muscle as we trust our gut instinct and perceptive heart. There are many different emotions that leave us feeling drained and unexcited about life. Intuitively we can sense that there is an imbalance, but we may not have personal tools or experience to recognize where the energy leak or imbalance is coming from. I have witnessed this depletion as physical sensations such as a heavy heart, unexplained emotions, irritation, and avoidance. It is my curiosity and my deep sense of 'wanting to figure it out' that propels me to quiet my mind enough, so I may listen to my intuitive voice. Creating space and time to go on a walk, meditate, dance, or pull weeds in the garden is usually enough to connect to my intuitive self-love. Everyone experiences energy leaks, which could be otherwise called worry, overthinking, or distraction from the present. The leaks happen when life presents us with situations that do not have a clear resolution or loved ones who are in constant need of your support. We can intuitively feel that a boundary needs to be created for your own self-worth. A situation may need outside guidance or a new collaboration as an exercise of self-compassion and desire to live with less stress. The moments when we lean into our challenges with a strong sense of love and worthiness, we discover that they are much more of a portal to healing than realized.

Sometimes our greatest acts of self-love are the moments when we realize we have made a mistake or acted unjustly and are willing to admit our wrongdoing and apologize. If we are a conscious person, we can feel when we are out of balance and our intuitive self-love is willing to sort it out. This can be messy, raw, and vulnerable, but enriching in the end. It is a stepping down from the need to be right, a pause to check on our built-up ego or a recognition of poor communication that supports the exercising of humility and grace. When we soften enough to feel the truth of what is bothering us, we discover the power of vulnerability.

Intuitive self-love can be as simple as cleaning your own kitchen when you are feeling ungrounded or spending quality time with a friend when something inside you just knew they were struggling. Intuitive self-love has its own heartbeat, which pulses, warms, and longs to be infused into one's daily life. It is a recognition of ancient wisdom that lives in our cells.

Contracted self-love

Contracted self-love is the inner shadow that is sneaking around your system with inadequate visions for you. Our bodies may even posture in a contracted way as we slump our shoulders or coil in to protect our hearts. Contracted self-love quietly tilts and allows all our gorgeous vital energy to leak out, leaving us in a state of feeling inadequate or fearful. We all have experienced some version of this contraction. It has the power to leave us stronger and more connected to the inner fire of our will to transform.

Once, years ago, I felt contracted and unable to function any longer within my stubborn thought patterns. If my husband was slow to get work projects and I was fed up, I would work twice as hard, and take care of our son and everything else in between, until I would literally crash and go to bed at 6:00 pm. This happened several times a year, not always due to the lack of work but because of my lack of trust. Finally, I made an appointment with my shamanic friend to help me uncover this pattern.

I had no idea what would surface in this shamanic healing session, but I was willing to follow her lead. I was laying on the massage table in a warm yurt while she did some tracking. Her questions and inquiries led me to recall memories of being an infant about 6 months old, with a serious case of pneumonia. I had to be put in an oxygen bubble for three days without my parents touching or holding me. Though I would have died without this treatment, the sense of abandonment had unknowingly entered my system. I was able to recall distant memories of looking out through thick, blurred plastic, surrounded by a sterile environment. My mom and dad were twenty-year-old new parents, feeling helpless and worried.

This experience left an imprint on my soul. The few days without physical contact stole my trust in the universe. This moment, at such a formative age, impacted how I would operate in my adult life. It created the thought pattern that I needed to work hard and do everything myself to survive.

In actuality, when we trust in the universe, we can connect to a deeper state of flow and abundance! The healing session was a turning point in shifting from contracted to expanded self-love. Even though I was able to retrieve this part of my soul and regain my sense of trust, there have been moments of rebounding back to feeling a victim within my own life. This is the dance of self-love. This is the turning point of acknowledging that there is no set destination.

Self-love is a living, breathing vibration that produces frequencies that shift from resonance to dissonance and across the spectrum between. In a sense, self-love has a wildness that swirls in the wind. If you are on a healing path, you have most likely danced with this dynamic. We all have layers of inner discovery that take charge in our lives and become the lens we look through. In my moments of healing experienced in the yurt, I was able to shift an internal belief that helped clear that particular lens that I saw the world through. When these moments happen, we may sense a profound turning point toward inner contentment that visits us for a day, a weekend, or is life-long and life-changing. Studying and practicing within the medicine wheel, which is rooted in Peruvian Inca Shamanism, has been a fast track to clearing deep roots of fear and fantasy over recent years. During Covid, I was traveling through the wheel for the second time and my teacher invited us to place the triangle of disempowerment on ourselves instead of in our relationships.

This was a profound turning point to recognize that my inner critic is the perpetrator and self-doubt stems from my inner victim, while the girl that just wants to run away from it all is my inner rescuer. Oftentimes, when we are in a contracted cycle of self-love, we are caught within the triangle.

The awesome thing about recognizing the triangle of disempowerment is that we can learn tools and techniques to step out of it...to gain our energy back and feel empowered.

Expanded self-love

"The cultivation of positive emotions, including self-love and self-respect, strengthens our inner resources and opens us to a broader range of thoughts and actions. In turn, we gain trust in our resilience and the ability to face whatever surprises life may throw our way. Indeed, life can be stressful, with periods of peril, but we can have confidence in our capacity to meet it, instead of being torn apart by it."

—**Sharon Salzberg,** from *REAL LOVE: The Art of Mindful Connection*

In the above excerpt, Sharon Salzberg expresses her interpretation of psychologist Barbara Fredrickson's theory of positive emotions, called 'broaden and build.'

I love this notion as we dance and turn towards expanded self-love. Living here, we are in rhythm with life, we are the wisdom keepers and we have learned to co-create rather than control. I think it is safe to say that we all experienced some level of challenge and hardship during the Covid-19 shutdown and precarious re-openings. The experience had me sifting through all the layers of self-love I have mentioned, exercising my new resilience again and again as a healing artist and dance/yoga studio owner.

I had already spent more than twenty years of wild entrepreneurship in small mountain towns. How could I possibly be stretched any further? A year into the wild wave of wondering whether I could ride the current, I stepped into an online yoga teacher training with Shiva Rea. I always wanted to study with her, and now I could—in my living room! I took two years to study, integrate, and feel the internal shifts that her offerings had on my nervous system. I was able to tap a deeper wellspring of love and re-energize my mystic heart with this practice. I was one of those who contracted Covid in late 2020. I suppose I had a form of long hauler symptoms, as I noticed

I became anxious more easily and my incessant worrying about my son seemed out of balance. Shiva Rea's training coincided with my desire to have a practice which met my inner need to downshift and be in the flow of life. Shiva introduced me to a new language that met my body's wish so I could claim my vertical power from the ancient lineage of yoga and dance. I noticed the need to meet my clients from a deeper place of love and engage my studio teachers with a vibration of support to stay on their path. I also claimed myself as a community leader with the message to keep rising.

The beauty of my lifestyle is that, while I am a student, I can integrate as I teach my WildCore movement classes, and encourage dancing and moving our energy as the path to amplifying aliveness. The world keeps turning and the expanded state of self-love continues to show the way.

We get to choose to turn toward our fears with love or turn away and run. Thich Nhat Hanh so beautifully wrote, "Wherever you go, there you are." The art of dance is so powerful as an outlet to express all the worries, the wonders, the wild, and the free. Our bodies get physically strong in all of this dancing, too! We condition to feel and prepare our hearts to perceive more clearly, so we may align with the magic of our intuition and sense the force that Star Wars so creatively revealed. In the movie they called it 'the force' and the chosen Jedis would receive more training to understand the life force that was moving through them. I know that many of us are Jedis in disguise as mothers, artists, healers, teachers, and housewives.

Dancing with self-love invokes curiosity and invites in the playful nature of discovery while we are alive. We are constantly expanding and contracting as we breathe, so of course we will continue to expose layers of self-love. One day we are expanded and in love with everything as one long inhale of fresh mountain air. The next day we may be challenged to the point of contracting inward and full of tears, only to expand into the next full breath.

The body is incredibly intelligent and when properly nourished, strengthened, and connected to the natural world, we will experience a profound sense of wholeness or inner holy ground that we want to bow to every day. The key to self-love comes in codes which the layers of instinctual, intuitive, contracted, and expanded can support you to unveil. If you keep stoking your inner heart-fire with the activities and passions that spark your YES, you will discover your own unique, twirling path to an incredible inner resource of courage and the determination to forgive yourself over and over if you need to, so you can take those first dancing steps to the freedom you find when you live in alignment with the keys to self-love.

BRIETTA LEADER

Brietta is a teacher of dance in its many forms of healing, prayer, play and conditioning. She grew up as a dancer and discovered her path as a healing artist in 2001, while traveling in Asia. The combination of Brietta's devotion to the dance, her gypsy spirit, family roots, and passion to support herself and others into an embodied conscious awakening has birthed her own trademarked movement form called WildCore™ Movement. Her years of study as a conscious dance leader and mentor for Soul Motion® began to blend her years as a Nia® Teacher, Massage Therapist, Shamanic student, devoted yogi, pranic healer, reiki practitioner, apprentice to mother-nature, energy enthusiast and performer. All of which contributed to WildCore's development.

In Brietta's first book, *WildCore: 12 Keys to Unlock Your Untamed Expression,* she shares vulnerable stories and the global adventures that led her to find her wild core, and asks you to reflect on your own initiation of the elements and your own wild beauty.

Brietta loves to inspire self-healing through movement and offers classes, workshops, online programs, co-creative retreats and performances to her hometown of Sandpoint, Idaho, surrounding areas and internationally.

Learn more at **wildcoremovement.com** and on Instagram: **@wildcoremovement**

Dancing with the Layers of Self-Love

You are invited to take a movement journey through the four layers of self-love described in "Turning Toward Self-Love."

Brietta will gently guide you through simple movement mudras that invoke the layers of your instinctual love, intuitive love, contracted love, and expanded love. Through movement, we are better able to connect to our deepest wisdom and allow the space and freedom for that expression to inform all of the different aspects of ourselves. Brietta's playful nature will support this exploration of movement and will illuminate the energy of love that is available to everyone.

Access at: **https://mailchi.mp/94a87dd9b60b/ turning-toward-self-love**

CHAPTER 3

From Near Death, We Rise Up!

By Maria A. Rodriguez

"Maria! Maria! He's not going to make it, Maria! We're losing our George, Maria! We're losing our George!"

As my sister sobbed between her words, my chest squeezed so tightly I could barely squeak out an, "Oh my God." She said my oldest niece was joining them in their home so that she and her three girls could be together when they received word that their father was gone. When the call ended, I stumbled up the stairs and into the shower, caught between unbearable pain and shocked numbness. I closed my eyes, letting the hot water wash over me, trying to reach the cold dread moving through my body.

Suddenly, I began seeing a vision of a car caravan of family and friends circling the hospital three times. I saw us shining healing light toward him and the medical staff, surrounding them in that 360° way. I heard us finishing with, "And so it is. And so it is. And so it is. Amen. Amen. Amen." I wasn't sure what that was all about since I was expecting a call any minute with the horrid news that he had passed.

It was the morning of April 2, 2020. We were about two weeks into the Covid lockdown in the United States. My sister had to make the awful decision to drop off her husband at the emergency room doors when she could barely wake him up anymore. Those were the days when some hospitals had been converted to Covid-only treatment centers. Loved ones were not allowed to visit. Covid had been running through my sister's family before most even knew what it was. My brother-in-law, George, who was only 56 years old, had been placed on a ventilator in an induced coma soon after he was admitted.

George is the kind of guy who always leaves an impression, be it friendly annoyance, affection, or, often, a combination of the two. As a result, he inspired prayers from many family members and friends, along with their family and friends. Despite the abundance of prayers, exceptional medical care, and supreme advocacy from his wife, he had yet to improve. My niece even began a Caring Bridges network the day before. She was receiving and relaying our short, encouraging, loving videos so the hospital staff could play them for him to (hopefully) hear. All we were seeing on the news was the Covid death count dramatically rising around the country and the world. We couldn't help but think that he would become another statistic.

The previous afternoon, I shared his critical condition in one of my ladies' circles, The Radiance Queens (named as such for the Radiance mastermind program where we met). One of the queens, Rima, had described a recent mystical experience while recovering from Covid. She had been shown in that spiritual way how to do remote healings with the Egyptian essential oils she often used. The healings entailed using specific oils in a grid pattern, calling upon feminine deities, and other energetic symbolism. When Rima heard about George, she immediately knew she was to offer this healing, even though she had never done it before, had never met George, and lived over 1700 miles away. That evening when she asked George's soul permission to do the healing, her discernment pendulum moved in a way that was not the usual yes or no she expected. Since it was inconclusive, Rima had me ask my sister for permission as his proxy, which my sister promptly gave.

I expected Rima to do the healing the next morning, as it was late by the time I gave her my sister's reply, the same day of my sister's distress call. My cousin, Vivian, had called me soon after my shower, having heard the same news. Neither of us had received an update. I wondered whether I should tell Rima not to bother with the healing, but something stopped me.

Ninety minutes past my sister's call, Rima messaged me to say she was doing George's anointing now and asked me to join her in seeing him feeling the healing benefits. I still felt compelled not to interrupt her with the news and to join her as she had asked.

In the meantime, Vivian had asked her husband to reach out to his long-time associate for healing suggestions…a man whom she had always kept at a distance because of his seeming affinity for Santeria, which Wikipedia describes as "…an Afro-Cuban religion merging 'the traditional Yoruba religion of West Africa, the Catholic form of Christianity, and Spiritism.'"

He suggested we light white candles while visualizing George being healed. Vivian didn't have white candles, but I remembered I had recently bought four white Miraculous Mother Mary/ Maria Milagrosa candles. I began creating an altar on the kitchen table as soon as we ended the call. My 9-year-old daughter, Bianca, was drawn to what I was doing and asked to help. Even though we had never done a healing ritual of this kind, we were called to place two round straw placemats, with the top one overlapping the bottom one. She and I then placed the candles in a pattern, with three in an arc on the top mat and one in the center of the bottom mat. My eyes were then drawn to our window ledge. Eight days earlier, we had gone to Lake Michigan for my birthday and gathered some stones now lined up on our ledge. Bianca and I began placing them on the mats, and before I knew it, we had created two concentric stone circles around the main candle, with three larger stones closely surrounding it. We then lit the candles while envisioning George being healed.

Meanwhile, Rima had asked me if everything was okay since I had not responded. I shared the horrible news we had received three hours earlier and how I wasn't sure if he was still alive. Rima continued working with him, being called to beam rainbow energy toward him, directing healing to each chakra with its corresponding color, and asked that I do the same. I shared a photo of the altar Bianca and I had created. She shared her oil grid, exclaiming, "OMG. You did four and three and the two concentric circles just like me!"

Whereas she had his name printed in purple in the center, we had the main candle representing him. Full body tingles coursed through us. Further

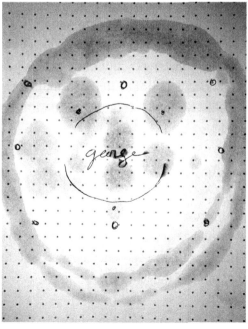

emboldened and encouraged, she continued to receive incredibly detailed Guidance. This included blowing into his lungs energetically, drawing a ring of Frankincense oil to protect him from spirits in the hospital, and adding four drops of her blood with its Covid antibodies. Weird, yes…but we were finding barriers dissolving left and right when it was a matter of life and death.

Then I received the news from my sister. A huge amount of mucous had loosened and been suctioned from George's chest. He went from an oxygen level of 30% that morning to the highest it had been during his six-day hospital stay at 96%! Still in critical condition and on the vent, but it went from near death to this. The feeling of being touched by grace was almost overwhelming. We all realized, however, that he was still in danger. Most were not surviving being on a vent for long, and there was now the additional concern of whether he had suffered brain damage from the loss of oxygen.

I shared this miraculous news with Rima and my deep gratitude for her generous and sacred contribution. She was overjoyed and yet knew he wasn't out of the woods. When I shared my caravan vision, she immediately saw us beaming the same rainbow light toward George while we encircled the hospital in our cars. She sent that message right at 11:11 am her time and 1:11 pm my time…simply stunning given that this master number is often seen at a time of spiritual awakening and deepening belief in the power of our thoughts and prayers.

Rima also shared a photo of a Sri Yantra—a Hindu mystical diagram. She had been called to draw one days earlier during her quarantine recovery. She discovered it only when she saw purple ink bleeding onto the sheet of paper with George's healing grid and lifted the page to see what had caused it. It turns out it was beneath George's anointing page and making itself known. Rima suggested I print an image of one from the internet to place on the car dashboard during the healing caravan. With these continued blessings, we felt part of something far bigger than what we could express in words and yet felt so deeply in our hearts and spirits.

This feeling was amplified when Rima and I discovered we were both struck that same evening by the NDE (Near Death Experience) aspect

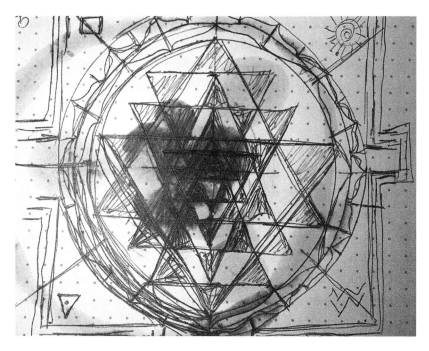

of this. My 16-year-old daughter, Cassie, had been sharing social media posts with me the last several days from young people writing about NDEs unrelated to Covid. It was as if she had been preparing me to remember what I already knew about NDEs. Rima realized we were going to have thousands of people across the globe waking up from NDEs, with all the wisdom that comes from touching into the other side of the veil, as a result of this virus. And how this was likely to play a big part in shifting our consciousness as a species. She was profoundly touched by what a massive act of selfless service this was from the NDE patients. I was struck by how it was the same for their loved ones, given their vast fear and suffering.

While I felt at ease when talking with Rima about my healing caravan vision, I was far more reluctant to run it past my sister for several reasons. First, my sister had a falling out decades earlier with the Catholic church where her wedding had taken place, and that seemed to affect her relationship with religion in general. She had also kept her distance from the mystical happenings of 1997, when spiritual forces blew into my life, changing its course forever.

Although I had come out of the closet spiritually in 2008, she and the rest of our extended family and family friends knew much less about the extent of my spiritual growth and leadership than my personal and professional friends, like Rima, did. In addition, my vision contained elements beyond the traditional Judeo-Christian world we were raised in. This, combined with my tendency to avoid shame and rejection, had me all frozen up. Our cousin, Vivian, however, insisted that I share this divine guidance since I had received it on their behalf. Absorbing her encouragement, I finally overcame enough of my fears and shared my vision, albeit quite uncomfortably. My sister, being broken wide open by this crisis, instantly agreed. We planned to do a trial run of the caravan the next afternoon to see if it was feasible. If all went smoothly, we would invite the entire support community to join us the following day.

When I opened my email the next morning, I was shocked to discover that it was National Rainbow Day! I don't know about you, but this was something I had never heard of before then—another small miracle, given that we were about to do the trial run using rainbow healing light. Then, I remembered that I had received a rainbow vision years earlier! Well, actually, a dear friend immediately saw my vision in rainbow colors just as I was describing it—in just the way my healing caravan vision became a rainbow healing caravan at Rima's suggestion. Another example of how, together, we are stronger!

That particular vision had come in response to a client's question about whether my Soul Speak circles were anti-Christian, as she was worried that participating would interfere with her faith. I paused before answering… practicing the spiritual discernment I teach and facilitate. What came to me was this:

> *The short answer is that the circles are not Christian or non-Christian. They transcend the level of religion and are centered on universal spirituality. Participants from different faiths report their faith as being enhanced rather than threatened or weakened.*
>
> *The long answer emerged through an image of a circle made up of "bridges" leading to the same center, each bridge representing one of the colors of the rainbow. But these bridges*

are not normal in shape. The much shorter hump of each bridge is at the tail end, leading to a higher central plane, rather than at the middle of each bridge.

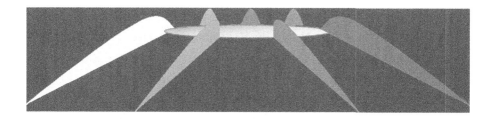

Now imagine each bridge representing a different faith and yet leading to the same center. This higher sanctum is Universal Spirituality—what all faiths have in common and what transcends all faiths. The higher hump part contains the unique aspects of each faith that enrich us all regardless of our faith, thus being one part of the whole of Universal Spirituality. When we open to them all, we are led to greater wholeness, higher wisdom, and a sense of oneness. Most of us begin our spiritual journey on one of these bridges, which can remain a central part of our identity and faith even as we ascend to this broader plane.

Upon hearing this, Rima felt confirmed in her sense that we had been preparing for this whole experience our whole lives. We were in awe of the timing of George's miraculous turning point; the moment we tapped into sacred wisdom from "different colored bridges" such as Hinduism, Buddhism, Egyptian, and Spiritism, to join with the Judeo-Christian ones already present through loved ones' prayers. God only knows what really happened. More may have been occurring in that moment within the larger community and on the other side of the veil. However, with these interfaith healing rituals now being linked to the previous interfaith vision, it was as if, through incorporating a broader spirituality, we activated the power of that Universal Spirituality center...of the one heart which unites us all. Also, I couldn't help but see how the concentric circles of this vision mirrored the healing grids Rima and I had intuitively created for George! At the very least, the rainbow aspect of the healing was being deepened and highlighted as we prepared for our first mini-Rainbow Healing Caravan.

The trial run was so emotionally and spiritually powerful that my niece immediately sent out word to everyone that we were hosting a caravan at the hospital at 5 pm the next day, Saturday, the 4th. She explained that her dad was still in critical condition, still on the vent. She requested that we play some of her dad's favorite songs—like Led Zeppelin's "Black Dog!"—a prayer or anything else of our choice as we drove around three times. Thank goodness for the rainbow synchronicities, as they gave me the courage to also add, "George received a special healing the day before, which you can join us in continuing if you'd like. It's simply sending him waves of rainbow-colored light and love energy while encircling the hospital three times. To anchor it further, we can end by saying, 'And so it is' and/or 'Amen' three times. A little weird, I know...but just in case this healing was part of the impact yesterday, we can build on that!"

Many of us were independently inspired to create posters. My husband, two daughters, and I made one where we each took one of the corners, colored our own rainbow with a personal message, and wrote in huge bubble letters in the center, "WE LOVE YOU, GEORGE." We were also inspired to include the medical staff in our blessings and prayers. We could not have predicted what would happen next.

When my sister shared with the medical staff what we were doing, they were beyond excited. They were waiting at the window of George's room as over twenty cars began arriving between 5 and 6 pm. They had post-it notes on the window with messages of gratitude for us. We saw them waving and taking photos and videos as we began getting out of our cars, holding up our posters while looking up at them. Some of the cars had posters taped to the rear windows with messages for George and for them. We had no idea what an impact we'd have on the medical staff, bringing hope, love, and even joy, at a time when they were mostly experiencing loss.

At 6:17 pm, my sister led the caravan with my three nieces and their four dogs in the car. You could see arms waving out of car windows and hear rock music blaring or words of encouragement being shouted out. We had the Sri Yantra printout on our dashboard as we drove around beaming rainbow light. We later learned George's doctor was telling George all about it right when it was happening, despite his still being unconscious.

I sent Rima the photos and video of the caravan. She cried tears of joy and love, so touched by my family's act of love. So inspired, she was hoping people would start doing this everywhere. Then she declared, "You are a high priestess, Maria, leading your people in love!" At the time, I could not take that in, as you can imagine. I was still reeling from watching my vision come to life in such a vibrant, potent, loving way. My niece posted the next day, "Day 9 in the hospital. Day 19 since symptoms started. Day 4 of good news! EVERYTHING is moving in the right direction!"

There were several more long days of breathing trials as they tried weaning George off the vent, with an especially bad reaction to reducing his sedation on April 7th. My sister kept fearing he wouldn't wake up. Rima worked with him again for quite a while the next morning. She kept hearing the Lynyrd Skynyrd song "Freebird" playing in her head: "I'm as free as a bird and this bird you cannot change." About an hour later, my niece posted an update that her dad was doing dramatically better, now fluttering his eyes and his oxygen dependence being almost at the 40% level needed to remove the vent. However, they needed him to wake up more fully, so everyone was on pins and needles. The longer it went, the higher the fear of brain damage became.

We were reassured and awed, however, by the amazing rhythm and weave that had been established. I would pass on to Rima the specific challenges my sister would share and she'd focus on those in her anointing energy work while continuing to confirm that it was his choice whether to stay or go, and then my niece would post an update that he had improved in that area! The rainbow part of the healing had also taken on a life of its own, as reflected by the rows of rainbow-colored hearts and rainbow emojis sprinkled liberally throughout our WhatsApp messages. On the 12th my sister actually took over the Caring Bridges update to post: "Our prayers and woo-woo are working! His mental capability is increasing (even trying to pull out the tube). Still with a fever but vitals good. Please keep praying and woo-wooing." Looking back, I see how we were all rising and shining at a level we never had before.

My sister and nieces kept on caravaning every night, with a few different cars joining them each time, including ours. After a harrowing week, George improved in bigger leaps. He was able to get off the vent, leave ICU, and start PT and OT! Thankfully, none of our worst fears about brain damage were realized. Words could not express the depth of our gratitude. We knew there was a long recovery road ahead and yet we couldn't help but feel the radiant presence of the holiest of grace.

My niece planned a community-wide Celebration Caravan on the 19th. This time George would be in a wheelchair at the window. He was discharged on the 25th! On the way home, my niece posted a photo from a family friend with the caption, "LUCKY RAINBOW FOR MR. WINK COMING HOME!" That's right…a frickin' rainbow.

Although George couldn't recall any of the ICU staff who cared for him during his three weeks on the vent, he was well-known amongst them as a Covid miracle of that time—much to his overwhelming surprise—and was greeted as such during his follow-up visits. They told him time and time again, often with tears in their eyes, that they had never seen a family and community quite like his. After a long, grueling rehab, he was able to walk his oldest daughter down the aisle at her wedding the following year… without a dry eye in the place!

On my end, this was just the beginning of continued and much-needed encouragement, from both the human and heavenly realms, to step out in my priestess self. Prior to Rima calling me a High Priestess, as a clinical social worker, I had never thought of myself in such terms. Since then, I have officiated my niece's wedding, published a sacred text, *From Barriers to Bridges: A Treatise,* and I even went on an "Avalon Remembered" priestess pilgrimage in Glastonbury.

I was born amid a near-death experience in which my mother reached up to a higher spiritual realm to help save her. It's conceivable then that the pronouncement and public emergence of the priestess part of my Greater Identity occurred when I reached for a higher plane during another near-death experience. Perhaps my priestess calling is "From near death, we rise up!" and this story can serve as inspiration for rising up.

Rising up to the universal spiritual realm which unites all faiths and all sentient beings. Rising up into our Greater Identity, overcoming our fears to do so. And rising up in terms of the psychological, spiritual, and social change paradigm shifts I call the Seven Bridges to Higher Consciousness. These teachings coalesced in a vision I had several years ago of an hourglass layered with these seven bridges. As I write this, I now see them as rainbow-colored bridges helping us evolve so we can rise up. The colors span from red at the bottom to violet at the top, from the bottom psychological healing layer of Breaking our Toxic Shame Cycles to the top spiritual growth level of Leading a Spirit-Driven Life—both so strongly reflected in this turning point story. For you can see how many of us overcame some of our toxic shame avoidance tendencies, thus allowing Spirit to guide the way.

MARIA A. RODRIGUEZ

Twenty-five years ago, spiritual forces blew into Maria's world, changing the course of her life forever. Mystical happenings led to a major relationship change so she could be united with the love of her life, Lou, and have his children (two daughters, Cassie and Bianca). Maria experienced a profound spiritual awakening, along with many who witnessed these happenings. She was then guided to make an unexpected turn professionally, leaving her beloved police social work career of fifteen years to develop a private counseling practice. Maria was soon jolted awake to the words *Sacred Spaces—within us, between us, around us*...a new name and unique direction for her work. As she became further aligned with her path and purpose, her sense of wholeness, aliveness, peace, and joy grew thus inspiring her to guide others to do the same.

Over time, this evolved into *Seven Bridges to Higher Consciousness—fundamental shifts to our way of thinking, being, living, and relating.* She continues to be in awe of the profound psychological healing, spiritual growth, social change, and even miracles these shifts tend to facilitate. Maria developed Cour de

Grace, LLC as an online forum to further her dream of an evolution revolution based on these empowering paradigms for living. She envisions a wisdom school and social movement, leading to a world where these become our mainstream mindsets and skill sets. Maria's unusual evolutionary perspective was displayed in the Chicago Tribune; her impassioned Letter to the Editor about injustice and the police, which garnered praise and thanks from both ends of the political spectrum.

Her book, *From Barriers to Bridges: A Treatise*, is a heartfelt plea and blueprint for our personal and collective evolution. Maria is devoted to healing ourselves, our relationships, our systems, and our communities; thus unleashing the power of Grace in the world. Her message to all beings: *Rise up. Be brave. Choose to evolve (and in turn, help the world evolve). The Entire Universe is rooting for you!*

"Claim Your Birthright"
PDF & Audio Recording

You have a right to access your Soul's Guidance and to live in accordance with it. Claiming this birthright becomes easier to do, the more we learn about what Guidance is, how it works, where we're blocked from receiving it, and why it matters...for us and for the world.

With this audio recording, you can practice one of the dialects of this Language of Spirit, clearing and widening your channel to receive. It is the very same Receiving Meditation I regularly practiced years ago, which helped pave the way to more readily access visions and guidance like the ones appearing in my Turning Point story.

No matter where you are on your spiritual evolutionary journey, claiming more of your birthright can enhance your healing, enrich your relationships, and empower you to make inspired choices—leading to your more authentic identity and soul-aligned life. May we all continue to rise up...and co-create miracles.

Visit **www.courdegrace.com** for more on rising up in these ways and to receive your free PDF and audio recording of **CLAIM YOUR BIRTHRIGHT: Light Up your Life with your Soul's Guidance as Healer and Navigator** (available on the Turning Point Stories tab of my website.)

CHAPTER 4

The Body Under the Floor: Resurrecting My Lost, Feminine Essence

By Dr. Michelle Ten Klooster

I'm back in my grandmother's house. It's dark, and there's a rank stench of decay penetrating the air. The curtains are closed, boxes are packed, and there is an emptiness that consumes me. I think about my Nan and I can still see her sitting in her favorite thread-worn armchair, drinking her milky tea in the same cup and saucer she always used. The familiarity of it brings up emotion and pain because I miss her so much. I sit down in the chair opposite hers, overcome by emotion and I imagine her there, smiling and offering up some wisdom in the way only she can. I smell her, I hear her, and I feel the touch of her warm, soft, crinkled skin on my cheek.

Sitting there in this emptiness, I begin to hear a faint noise. Is it a mouse or something stuck inside the kitchen? I stand up and walk around, looking for where this sound is coming from. The sound suddenly becomes louder and more urgent. I enter Nan's weather-beaten makeshift conservatory, and I realize what I'm hearing is a heartbeat. The sound becomes almost deafening and I'm experiencing it vibrationally as it pulls me physically and energetically toward it, as if I'm being sucked into a vortex. I'm scared; my palms are sweaty and my throat is dry. I want to run away but I can't—it won't let me—and even if I could run, my legs are like jelly.

There is something pulling me closer. It's stronger and more powerful than me, a feeling that I can't ignore no matter how much I want to. I speak out loud, "I can hear you, but please leave me alone, I need to get on with my life. I don't have time to deal with you…please go away…please just leave me alone."

I know this place; it's a memory of something that happened long ago… something I had tried to forget. My heart starts to beat faster and my body is feeling the familiar fear that has become part of my everyday life since I was little. She haunts me and follows me no matter how hard I smile and try to numb her out.

There is a body under my feet. She lies down there, probably a bag of bones by now. After all these years, no one has found her. I was sure they would when they dug up the old conservatory to replace it. This is my last chance to move the body so I won't get caught. After all these years I had waited with bated breath and fear that I would be found out, and how my life would be torn apart by anyone finding her.

My Nan was the only one who knew, and she had helped me bury her, helped me keep my secret. I looked around and I see my Nan standing there with her spade and garden wellies on saying, 'Michelle, it's time to dig her up.' I scream out and try to stop her but she is already striking the ground. The floor falls in as I knew it would because of the secret room that is hidden underneath. I slowly look down and I see the dark blanket thrown over what now is a bag of bones, the remains of the girl buried and lost to this life. All the experiences and life never lived because I had killed her, ended her life before it had really begun. I had stolen her dreams. I would like to tell you that it was an accident that I didn't mean to, but I will not lie to you…it was premeditated, cold, and calculated and I have spent most of my adult life justifying to myself why I did this. Now, I let myself remember, because I chose to forget and move on and start a new life, but now it's time.

Back then I knew what I wanted and trust me, nothing and no-one was going to stand in my way. It was me or her and she was wild and untamed with big out-of-the-box dreams and a big mouth. She threatened me with her girliness and inability to stay quiet or shut up—she always had to have the last word. She would always get me into trouble and say things that would humiliate or shock people; she didn't care what anyone thought about her. She was a loose cannon, and I did her a favor by killing her because she would never have survived this life. I was so scared she was going to ruin my life by being in it. There wasn't room for both of us, so I chose me, killed her, and buried her here and tried to forget that she had ever existed, or that I had done the unthinkable and ultimately unforgivable.

The familiar panic and fear mixed with regret and shame begins to consume me; her anger and pain begin to pull me into the angry open hole that I have re-opened. I feel her rage reaching out for me, like tendrils of a tree. I lose my balance and fall…I scream…

…and then I wake up.

This is a dream I've been having weekly for the past 20 years. The memory of her has haunted me for so long as well as the avoidant behavior that I've adopted to try and free myself from her.

Every time I wake up, my heart is beating so fast, I'm sweating, and I can feel all the emotions—I'm there in that house, locked into the past. The feelings have been so real that there have been times where I thought that maybe there was a dead body lying there and I actually *had* killed someone. I know this may sound crazy, but this is what starts to happen when we ignore our dreams and our soul—the messages start shape-shifting into the waking hours. For years, I would get up distract myself and try and do, think, and be anything other than what my dream was trying to show me.

My turning point story is one of remembrance—a haunting of my inner feminine, the lost part of myself that I'd buried away and tried to forget. But now I know that we never truly forget, that the body holds onto the parts of ourselves we disown, ignore, or are repelled by. The effort and energy to keep up the pretense, firstly to myself and then others, has cost me dearly.

The parts of myself long forgotten or disowned were never truly gone because energy and something that powerful can never be destroyed or held down forever—it always finds a way to flow, just like water. We keep our true feminine essence—our SHE—locked up inside our cells, and we forget that she was ever part of us, yet she is always there living and breathing within our DNA until she manages to break free. And then she comes for you like she did for me.

What I've come to learn is that when ignored, she manifests as illness or an event in life that ends up waking you up, stripping back the masks, and knocking over the picture-perfect life we've tried to create. She enters in full, bold, and loudly unapologetic, like the relative you try to pretend is not related to you.

She grabs you, pulls you to her, and stares you straight in the eye. You smell her, hear her, feel her, and that taste in your throat lets you know that you can no longer swallow your own poison. She is here, and she will not be ignored anymore. There is nowhere to hide, nowhere to run. She has you, and you are hers. She screams at you, letting you know that you are not really in control of anything which is ironic because half the time we try to control everything—oh, the goddess has a sense of humor! When you finally surrender and let her take the wheel, then you truly begin to live the life you came here to live.

My turning point was slow and stretched out over a period of 3 years. I had, by my superficial standards, made it in life. I had climbed the career ladder as a successful chiropractor with my own business. I was married with 4 beautiful children and was comfortable by society's standards. I had ticked all the boxes and I had the gold star, but the truth was, I was dying inside. Underneath my outward projection of perfection, my health was suffering. I had multiple breast cysts, two of which had needed surgery. I had debilitating PMS, and the icing on the cake was when I was told I needed to remove part of my cervix because cancer cells were spreading. It was as if all my female parts were failing me, letting me down. I was tired, physically, mentally, and emotionally and there was a burning rage simmering under the surface that would escape and explode from me at the most inconvenient times—and usually at the wrong people.

I had no joy and was unhappy, which made me feel guilty, always wondering why I wasn't happy with the life I had created. I had followed all the rules and yet, I still didn't feel good. So, I did what most women do in their forties when they find themselves at this place—I tried harder and aimed for more, thinking that would make me happy. I pushed myself to do and be better; I revved up on caffeine and numbed out with food and alcohol until I eventually hit a wall where my body was screaming so loud—the rageful feminine inside of me was crying to be let loose.

This recurring nightmare was my soul trying to get my attention, but I wasn't ready to see her or hear her. Couldn't she see how busy I was and that there was so much to do in my life? But that voice, that memory…wouldn't go away. The more I pushed the harder she pulled.

She was demanding that I listen, showing me what I needed to do yet I was creating aversions and distractions and running around like I was lost, pretending I was stuck. Being lost was a choice; I see that now. Lost was comfortable, I didn't have to do anything. It fed the illusion that I was a victim and that I had no power—that all this was happening *to* me when in truth, it was happening *for* me. My illusion was keeping me from living. It was creating a false sense of security. I needed to choose not to be lost anymore and I had to make a choice and follow my heart no matter how crazy my mind was telling me it was. The truth I now know is that as long as I am fully me, fully present, and connected to the divine, I will always find my way back to my soul.

During this time a quote from Jesus in *The Gnostic Gospel of Thomas* by Leloup came to me: "If you bring forth *that* within you, then *that* will save you. If you do not, then *that* will kill you."

I knew in that moment that digging up the lost parts of myself would save me and I also knew that if I didn't, I would die if not physically at first then spiritually and emotionally. I had to listen. No more hiding or pretending.

It was around this time that I began working with a priestess school where I trained to be a priestess and underwent some deep initiations into the feminine mysteries. The *13-Moon Mystery School* is a place that I had been called to for a very long time but I thought, as a doctor, it was too woo-woo for me, and I knew best—or so I thought.

During this time, I deeply embodied and re-wired my mind, body, and soul back into the ancient ways of the feminine. Through this journey, I began to remember who I was. I reclaimed the lost parts of me I had buried away long ago. During my time in temple, I was being shown again and again that my dream meant something, and I couldn't ignore the call any longer; it was my soul, my unconscious screaming at me.

And so, I began to journal and go on deep inner journeys into my body and soul. I began to feel that the invisible world was just as real as the visible. I spent more time going inward and started to question everything I did, who I really was, and what I truly wanted, with the biggest question being, "What is my purpose and why am I here?"

My soul search lead me on a sacred Mary Magdalene pilgrimage to France, where I visited sacred sites and I placed myself in a vortex of her energy. Whilst in the cave of Mary Magdalene, a woman from the group asked me to join her on a private tour of another cave that was 45 minutes up the mountain. She told me that she had been told by her guides to take me. Now, I'm not the type of person to just go with someone I barely know in a foreign country to a place I had never heard of before, but as she spoke, I knew in my body that I was meant to be there, right now in this time and place, and that this cave was a place my soul needed to visit.

The walk around the mountain was not for the faint-hearted. We had a guide who helped us navigate the rough terrain. We used ropes at times to secure ourselves because it was slippery, and there was a big drop to the side of us. My mental brain kept telling me I was crazy, "What am I doing?" Yet my soul knew the way, and it felt as if this cave was calling me home. Once we got to the cave, I realized instantly where we were—it was known as the "Cave of Eggs." The entrance is shaped like the opening of a yoni, so, it's sometimes referred to as the "Yoni Cave." We had to enter into the cave using a rope. Luckily, the guide had given us flashlights to wear on our head as it was deep and dark. The walls were damp, moist and smooth, contoured into multiple eggs. It was one of the most spectacular places I have ever experienced! It felt like I was inside the Great Mother's womb. Time stood still; it was as if I had been transported out of time and body. I felt home. I felt the feminine, the Mother—all the things I had tried to feel but couldn't embody before standing in this cave. She had called me back through timelines, called me home to Her—the lost piece of my puzzle, my soul...The little girl that was buried became reborn in that cave and I came out of it a different woman. I'd "remembered."

After this experience, I was led to study and embody the ways of the sacred feminine even more deeply. I studied sacred sexuality and went through an initiation called the "13 Gates of the Sacred Roses." I became a womb gatekeeper of ancient feminine mysteries while also pursuing my priestess studies.

Every month I was beginning to feel more alive. People could see the change in my body and my face—I even spoke differently. I now know in my bones that I am worthy of love just as I am. I don't need to prove or be anything. Love is available to us simply because we exist–and it doesn't need to be earned. My worth is not based on what I've done, how I look, or what I have. All the trying and pushing I had been busy with all those years now seemed so irrelevant, and were just distractions from the truth.

What was needed for my healing was to embody my truth and to extend love and light to all the places I had shut down, so I could experience pleasure as well as pain—and accept my shadow and light. This is what was needed to overcome the illnesses that had plagued me for years. Everything I had been looking for was there within me all along, yet I had been searching everywhere for it outside of myself. I felt like Dorothy in *The Wizard of OZ* when she looked down at her red slippers—awakened! I had to remove the blocks and switch it on to reawaken the dormant Shakti that was hidden and suppressed within me.

The following year, I went on another life-changing pilgrimage to Glastonbury, England—the site in the Arthurian legends called Avalon. A year earlier, I had trained in the Art of Anointing as a part of my priestess studies. When I become a scent priestess, I was given an essential oil to work with. My mentor shared that the oil of cedarwood "chose me." Metaphysically, cedarwood is grounding and is the bridge between the physical and spiritual. But when I was first received this oil, I felt completely deflated—my other sisters were getting all the "exotic" oils and I had been given cedar. I could feel the comparison welling up inside of me, being surrounded by mystical priestesses who, in my perception, were more magical. This experience opened my eyes to something I was missing and showed me how I was still looking outside of myself for validation, rather than from within.

You see, I love science and the body, but after 20 years of study and practice, I wanted to be and do everything spiritually. I believed that this was the path I was meant to be on; this was the way to get closer to my soul. Yet, in truth, I would sit in sister circles and feel like I was missing something, that my gifts weren't as strong, and I couldn't understand why I wasn't having visions like the other sisters. I felt embarrassed and lost, like I didn't belong.

In Glastonbury, we visited the white and red springs and the Tor, all of which touched me deeply, but there was something missing. Stuck between the worlds of the spiritual and physical, I was so fed up with myself, exhausted by my own negativity.

One day while wandering in Avebury around ancient tombs and stones, we came across a cave that had been used as a tomb thousands of years ago. Inside the cave, we began building an altar and meditating. I remember sitting there on the floor with my legs crossed and palms open, when suddenly, I was back in my dream in my Nan's house!

I can sense a younger version of me standing right in front of me, smiling and full of life. I smile, and I feel a surge of aliveness rise within me. Her form begins to change into an old crone. She is short, with the blackest eyes I have ever seen, wearing a gummy grin and bone necklace, and she is staring straight at me. I'm afraid, but then I see a twinkle behind her eyes and my whole body is released. She places two balls of white light into my hands. The light begins to move through my body, healing me and centering me in that moment. She then hands me her stick which is made of wood with a snake carved and coiled around its length. I see now that she was handing me back my power, my permission to be me. I heard the words "The way to the soul is through the body; embodiment will bring you home and be a bridge to light the way."

In that moment, I got it. The cedar tree, the bridge, and my strength were all symbols of my embodied wisdom—and I knew more about the body than most people! The physical, chemical, emotional, and spiritual body all had to be brought into balance to heal and awaken.

Most women I speak to spend their lives trying to get out of their body, control it, or turn it into something it's not. We've been conditioned to see the female body as something to be tamed—an enemy and inconvenience that is always letting us down. We spend time meditating and trying to reach new heights, bypassing the voice of our feminine body, ungrounded, missing half of the experience of our soul. For the body to rise, it must be fully grounded in the feminine. We must know our shadow before we are fully able to see the light.

The feminine has shown me that life is cyclical. Just like the caterpillar must die to become the butterfly, so must we die to the ways that are keeping us from who we truly are. The "not knowing"—the chrysalis—must be experienced before the butterfly can emerge. The underworld—our shadow—holds the gold. Rebirth always follows death and nature is our greatest teacher. She's always leaving us symbols and messages encoded in our environment and in the way our body communicates with us.

My body was *always* talking to me. Even when I stopped listening, she had to scream loud to get my attention, to wake me from the slumber I had fallen into that had become my life. Many of us are distracted, walking an unattainable line of perfection or simply numbing out because we are lost and spellbound by our own internalised patriarchal narrative. I have learned that the body will only be ignored for so long until she starts to wreak havoc to get our attention.

For so long, I believed my life had to look a certain way and be like everyone else's—and this was the illusion that has now been broken. My ability to hold space, and helping others to become more embodied, is my spiritual gift and purpose.

Embracing and trusting this has changed everything.

DR. MICHELLE TEN KLOOSTER

Dr. Michelle ten Klooster is a Chiropractor and Functional Medicine Practitioner. She is a healer, medical intuitive, and soul coach. She helps women midwife their souls back to life through sacred embodiment, reconnecting the mind, body, and spirit which she calls sacred feminine health/sacred women's health.

Her life's work is helping women build the bridge between science and the sacred. She weaves together modern science and ancient wisdom, teaching how healing and transformation can be experienced between these dualities.

She is a practicing chiropractor, coach, and priestess, teaching women's health and sacred sexuality whilst also being a womb keeper of the ancient feminine mysteries. In addition, she is a trained female health coach in practice for 15 years and is certified in the Conklin method of cellular cleansing.

Her life's work is to make the unconscious conscious through the power of the body, mind, and spirit. Michelle teaches women how to connect to their bodies and how to awaken to who they really are. She supports women with their hormones and life stages that require scientific and sacred modalities. She offers in-person and online workshops, group and private coaching, as well as hands-on healing sessions. She weaves together food, herbs, movement, ritual, energy work, and shakti activation. She believes that knowledge is power, and the power of the female body should be known to every woman and that all women have the right to feel at home in their body.

Michelle was born in Wales but has lived in the Netherlands for over 15 years with her husband Vince and their 4 children Olivia, Isabella, Sebastian and Emilia-lily.

FREE GIFT

Seasons of the Body: Attuning to the Cycles of Nature

Dynamic Life Skills is designed to guide you in remembering or discovering Easy-to-use tools to bring ease to your Central Nervous System and encourage greater alignment with Mind, Body, and Spirit. In other words, these tools will help you live in the center of the teeter totter, gently keeping balance even if the world is fluctuating wildly around you.

To access: **www.Drmichelletenklooster.com/tps**

Featured Author

CHAPTER 5

Divine Destiny…the Gift of Breast Cancer

By LeeAnn Wehr

"God, if you let me live, I'll help others heal."

Spoken in fear over 35 years ago, the night before my mastectomy. I remember this promise, as if I'd made it today. And so I invite you to join me on my healing journey.

Several months earlier my gynecologist recommended that I get a mammogram due to my "lumpy" breasts. So of course I did! A questionable spot led me to a consultation with a surgeon who said, "It's most likely a calcification, but I recommend a biopsy to be sure."

"Of course. Let's do it." Shortly after that, I sat alone in his office, believing it to be "just a calcification." Wrong—it was cancer! The surgeon suggested a mastectomy. I wasn't ready for that.

I searched out a second opinion—a panel of doctors and oncologists who suggested a lumpectomy. The original surgeon disagreed, but performed the lumpectomy. I anxiously awaited the findings. After what seemed like weeks, the results showed unclear margins, leading to another lumpectomy. This time, the waiting turned into almost two weeks when, finally a dear friend called the doctor's office for me. Now, that small calcification had begun to grow—diagnosis: intraductal carcinoma. The surgeon, without saying anything, allowed the *I told you so,* to hang in the room and said, "Time for that mastectomy. But don't worry; it won't hurt! Little did he know...

While waiting for that surgery, my husband and I took a weekend camping trip. Immersed in nature, I awoke with the realization that people die from cancer. I had been in denial—but right then, I chose life! The mastectomy required a couple of days in the hospital. Anesthesia and pain pills made me sick. Just get me out of here! My sweetheart swept me out of the hospital in a wheelchair, and we began the drive home.

At home, after so many procedures, the pain was intense. My parents and sister took a road trip to see that I was okay. Unfortunately, I spent a large part of that visit in bed, but their presence boosted my intention for healing.

I remember the horror of my first shower after removing the bandages when I viewed my concave half-chest—also climbing up the wall of our fireplace with my left hand to regain strength and use of that arm. After all I had to get ready for tennis season.

After my mastectomy, my substitute teacher gave me the name of a psychotherapist. I worked through my emotions about having cancer through biofeedback, polarity therapy, bodywork and meditation. *Why me? Why so young?* (I was 38!) I moved on and through the anger at my surgeon and his cold, uncaring treatment of me. I deserved better. I forgave. I cried. I screamed. I feared. I reached out and asked for support. I received. I searched. I released. I accepted. I learned to love myself more. I tried to stay positive. I struggled. I volunteered. I began healing.

Strength and courage filled my body cells, as the love and support of family, friends, students, an extraordinary husband, angels, and guides encouraged me and let me find my way...even though they didn't understand what I was doing or where I was going. And neither did I. I remained open and allowed information to come to me.

I had to fulfill my promise to God/Goddess, but how? I made up new rules as I went along. I listened to my inner self and began to find out what it was I wanted to do with my life. My priorities changed and my friends changed. Some fell away, because I was a threat to them and their own mortality, or they didn't know what to say, so they just stayed away. Others stepped forward and were there for me. I took charge of my life. Cancer empowered me. I began by becoming a volunteer for the American Cancer Society's Reach for Recovery program, which led me to four other local survivors who joined together in a support group.

One of the group members, a dear friend and fellow teacher passed on to another reality. I was with Ann during her final days, and her transition made me want to share and help other women go through this ordeal even more. I had to pass on the tremendous lessons I learned.

Healing emanates from the heart, and transpires on all levels of existence...the physical, mental, emotional, and spiritual. I believe most discomfort and disharmony begin at the emotional level, so clearing there was essential. I asked myself what a calcification might mean?? It was a hard, solid spot...was there hardness/grief/sadness in my heart chakra? I realized that I must develop more self-love...I began with this affirmation: *I love, approve and accept myself unconditionally, just as I AM,* which I repeated three times throughout the day.

Do you have any calcifications? How do you love yourself?

My process continues today, and I still cleanse, clear, align, harmonize and stabilize my energetic and body systems. As I grew spiritually, my awareness reached out and contributed to the healing of the Earth and all her inhabitants. We are indeed All One. I didn't have to wait until I felt "ready." I "knew" this was my destiny.

I am a lifelong learner...seeking knowledge, reading books, taking classes, and upgrading my skills. As I satisfied my curiosity and passion for learning, my path unfolded synchronistically. Initially, I discovered the work of Edgar Casey. My search intensified after my final surgery, and I inhaled books by Bernie Siegel, Louise Hay, Deepak Chopra, and Norman Cousins. There are so many more resources available today for you to explore. Some of my studies, considered more "out there" by the mainstream, led me to shamanism and Energy work.

I decided that the allopathic medicine practiced in the West was narrow-minded, focusing on healing only the physical symptoms. Many physicians didn't have the time or skill to look at a patient as a sacred being of light...

one who wants to be whole, to discover who they are, to know themselves on a deeper level, to find and follow their sacred path. This has shifted and, now, the market abounds with information written by open-minded, caring, compassionate doctors who realize the importance of treating the "whole" being rather than just the symptoms. I know traditional medicine has its place, but it is not the only answer. I trust a holistic approach that looks at all aspects of the individual.

I accepted cancer as a gift—an opportunity given to me. Before cancer, I dabbled and searched for who I AM, but not with the intensity I found in my own healing process. I passionately pursued my cure, choosing to live in the present moment. I set intentions each day to BE well, whole and perfect in body, mind and soul. Affirmations remain a vital part of my daily health and well-being. I have affirmations for each of my chakras, such as "I AM grounded, centered, focused and neutral in the game of control. My body is light, comfortable and pain-free. I love my body." These affirmations help open, stabilize and harmonize my red root chakra located at the base of my spine.

Early on, I began to ask to bring in Divine love in the form of light— often brilliant white or intense golden Christ consciousness light. As I learned to do this daily, I shared with others this easy and incredible way to connect with our Divinity. Just ask to open your crown chakra on the top of your head, and trust that you are receiving loving, Divine light. Ask, and you shall receive.

At times, I struggled to let go of fear, and to trust, believe and know that I was restored. I moved on. I became more aware of subtle energies, angels, fairies, and my connection with the animal, mineral and plant kingdoms. My intuition opened so that I hear, see, feel, and know, not only on the physical level, but also on an etheric level.

I don't remember strange, psychic occurrences as a young child. I grew up in a healthy, supportive environment, albeit with a strict Catholic upbringing. So, the appearance of an unknown being didn't startle me into an awakened state. Instead, I had to discover that my knowing has always been within. I became more aware through classes, meditation, connecting with nature, energy work, reading, meditating, practicing and teaching . To this day, I continue to maintain and enhance my spiritual connection. This closeness with our own Divinity is a unique experience for each of us. There is no "one" way to access this, but your own way.

Early in the 1990s, the word *Reiki* kept coming up for me in something I read or a conversation I had or overheard. The spell of this ancient, subtle form of hands-on relaxing, clearing and healing reached out for me. A visit to a psychic fair connected me with the woman who was to be my Reiki Master Teacher, Catherine Cole. In a few minutes, she helped me be aware of and liberate grief and sadness to which I had unknowingly clung. With its release, feelings of unconditional love flooded me, and great warmth and peacefulness saturated my body.

I experienced the first two levels of Usui Tibetan Reiki in a weekend class. Anyone can learn this process; studying anatomy or spending hours of training and practice is unnecessary. I learned about the body's anatomy and systems through continued practice and upgrading my skills. With the necessary attunement I became a clear, pure channel for spiritually guided life force energy. Reiki is one of the best tools available for self-empowerment and spiritual development. It brings me into a state of balance and harmony. It supports the natural ability of the body to heal itself. Reiki loosens blocked energy and promotes a state of total relaxation. I can channel this Divine energy for the rest of my life. One of the things I love about Reiki is that I can offer it to myself *and* others.

As this universal energy moves through me, my hands tingle and heat up as a physical signal of the intensity and beauty. I am a channel, and I wanted to share this. My living room floor opened as the first place for this labor of love. I ignored the discomfort of kneeling and bending over to bring through life force energy. I received healing as I offered it to clients. If I woke up early or during the night, I began an energy session and it always calmed me, balanced me, and helped me go back to sleep.

As I continued to practice I began to see visions, to hear suggestions for herbs to use, a book to read, a crystal, and further treatments. I knew something that I hadn't known earlier. The warmth touches me as it streams through me and out my hands onto a patron. Whatever is revealed to me, I share with the client. Nothing surprises me, and I share whatever comes through. It doesn't have to make sense to me, I'm only the receiver and transmitter. The information given is for the client's interpretation.

I became more aware that I am not only physical but that I exist on many levels. I continued my studies and became a Master Teacher of three lineages of Reiki. But this was only the beginning! Other modalities popped up synchronistically for me to pursue, study, practice, and offer to others: Angel Therapy, Spiritual Response Therapy, Crystalline Consciousness Technique, ARCHES, EMF Balancing. All of these combined to raise my frequency, and assist me with my own healing so that I can support others on their journey to health and well being.

I believe in the saying, "Once a teacher, always a teacher." I expanded my teaching portfolio to include classes such as: "Discovering Your Seven Chakras," "Re-Awakening your Inner Goddess," "How to Connect with Angels" (which later expanded to include totems, Guides, and more), "A Journey into Wholeness," "Come Alive," "BE the Light," "The 4 Clairs," "How to Use a Pendulum," and more!

An early Reiki session:

I sit quietly, hands in prayer position, thumbs touching my heart, and ask for permission to do the session. I affirm and prepare myself before my client arrives.

I am a clear pure channel for spiritually guided life force energy, guidance, wisdom and understanding. I ask for the support of the most benevolent beings of healing, my Reiki Guides, and my High Self to offer the most potent healing possible today. I ask to heighten my psychic abilities and intuition so that I may bring forth any relevant and important information. For this, I AM most grateful; I surrender my will to Divine Will and ask to be free of ego and any attachment to outcome.

I clear the energy of the room, provide shielding and invoke the highest frequency healing guides to join us for the session, in ways exactly for the client's highest good.

After she arrives, we discuss how she's doing and her intentions for today's session. Then she reclines on my massage table, open and ready to receive. I move my hands slowly above and along her body as I smooth her aura, flicking away discord. I use my pendulum to check her chakras for imbalances. This gives me an idea of where the blocks to the open flow of life force energy are and some clues as to what's going on. Reiki is all-knowing, so it flows where it's most needed.

I place my hands on the top of her head as she lies on the table. "Just allow your crown to open and receive this Universal gift of love, light, and healing sent directly from God/Goddess." I already feel a shift as she unfolds and opens more to accept the vitality coming her way.

"Receive and accept this loving energy, and know that it's moving through your physical body, all your chakras, and your energy field to clear, cleanse, heal, balance and harmonize."

I'm drawn to work on her solar plexus. "Breathe deeply into your solar plexus...get in touch with this part of your body; open to the sensations. Are you aware of anything that may be holding you back from stepping into your full personal power?"

"I see myself as a limp, weak ballerina hanging from strings like a puppet drained of color and enthusiasm. I've given my power away. I'm afraid to stand up for myself. I don't feel worthy."

"Are you ready to let go of that fear and unworthiness?"

"Yes!"

"Let's work together using breath and intention to release and transmute it. Does the fear have a shape or form, a color? Is it solid, hard, or soft? What's it like?"

"It's black and slimy. It's moving around. It seems to have tendrils."

"Take a deep breath in with the intention to set this free with gratitude for the lessons you've learned...and now exhale forcefully through your solar plexus and see and feel it leave. We'll send it out to the edges of your energy field to be transmuted into loving, healing energy, high self esteem, and personal power...Big breath in...big release..."

"Again...Excellent...Again...Perfect...Once more to send out any debris." She unloads fear and unworthiness.

"Now, let's fill the void with bright, emerald green healing light. Allow yourself to take in as much as you want. Remember, this is not my energy, but Universal energy. Breathe in deeply. Receive, receive, receive…

"How are you doing?"

"My vitality is back. I'm not a puppet anymore. I'm alive and dancing freely."

We continue to assist her, releasing unforgiveness, and opening her heart to the love she deserves. I see Angels lifting her away on a pink cloud to travel and play on the beach. They anoint her with oils and offer her flowers. She swims with the dolphins. She remembers and recognizes her true essence and beauty.

This is a co-creative process. My clients benefit more when they participate through intention, dialogue, breath, conscious release, and then receive. Some come for an energy-balancing session because it feels good. It's so relaxing, and exactly what their soul seeks; they may even fall asleep. On a subconscious level, they open and heal. On a physical level they feel calm and peaceful.

Not only do I practice this ancient system, but I also teach others to channel it. Through the years, many students have come forward to study with me. Teaching these classes fulfills me, as I see the benefits expanding, the work extending, and love touching a greater number of participants. Those calling out for healing support far exceeds the number of practitioners. The effect radiates, spreading further and further in the world. Most study for their own benefit and the advantage of their family and friends. Only a few will actually have a public practice. I have had students use the energy to enhance their artwork, music, and gardens. They discover they can use it on plants and mechanical and technical devices.

My sessions today are very eclectic, as I ask for the perfect modality for each client and offer them an oracle card reading. Some clients heal by passing over to the next dimension as a final healing for this life time's physical body, while their soul is eternal. Teaching also enables me to keep my promise further. My journey of healing and teaching has taken me from Colorado to Mexico to Arizona and now to New Mexico. I invite you to step into *your* healing journey, no matter what shadows may lurk for you. I want you to know that I am here to support you on your sacred journey. You are never alone!

LEEANN WEHR, CRM, ATP, MA

LeeAnn Wehr, CRM, ATP, MA is a gifted facilitator and author. The experience of healing from breast cancer over 35 years ago propelled her to a higher level of functioning, learning and healing. And she realized her potential as a healer, first for herself, and then others. Her vast experience includes the following modalities; Usui Tibetan Reiki, Shakti and Parallel Reiki, Angel Therapy, Spiritual Response Therapy, Crystalline Consciousness Technique, and more.

LeeAnn draws from these various techniques to offer her clients in the United States, Latin America and Europe energy balancing that leads the body to its own healing on the physical, mental, emotional and spiritual levels. She has a strong connection to nature, the angelic realm and spirit. Angels help her to fulfill her greatest potential by leading her to the experiences that most benefit her and others.

LeeAnn holds a Master's degree in Linguistics and has traveled extensively in Latin America. She even got married at Machu Picchu in Peru! She's lived in Mexico where she co-founded a scholarship fund enabling young people to attend high school and college which is still very active. She's passionate about charities that support women and children.

In addition to individual therapy sessions, LeeAnn offers an assortment of classes in Reiki, Chakras, "Intuition (the 4 Clairs),"

"Awakening your Inner Goddess," "BE the Light," "Communing with Angels," and more. She currently resides in New Mexico, the land of enchantment, with her husband and precious yellow lab, Maggie. For more information visit: **www.leeannwehr.com**

LeeAnn's ebook, *Meditations and More to Awaken your 7 Chakras* is available on Amazon at **amazon.com/dp/ B00D614QB4.**

Each Sunday, LeeAnn listens to angels and her High Self to provide her with the theme for her weekly message. If you would like to receive it, please contact her at **angelhelp4u@msn.com.**

FREE GIFT

Chakra Affirmations

This set of affirmations for each chakra will allow you to select what resonates with you.

To access: Email LeeAnn at **angelhelp4u@msn.com** to request your copy of the Chakra Affirmations pdf.

CHAPTER 6

A Trillion Lifetimes

By BrahmanKyrie

The muffled sound of male voices filled my ears, and I could vaguely make out where I was. I had no idea what day it was or the time. It was overcast outside, which could mean early morning or sunset. I was never too sure. Moments like these were always disorientating; the brief intervals between excessive drinking and drug-taking were practically nonexistent.

Doing my best to open my eyes, I stared at the ceiling, trying to get my bearings and recall some of the details of the night before. I tried to lift my head off the pillow but couldn't. I had no doubt taken a handful of Xanax to get to sleep, so I surrendered instead and lay there staring at the ceiling. The room seemed grey in every sense of the word, and the feeling of isolation was palpable.

Breathing quietly through an open mouth, I tried to interpret what they were talking about in the living room. My nose was too sore to use for breathing as copious amounts of cocaine abuse had burnt the inside of my nostrils and my eyes would be swollen after gobbling down too many Xanax. I would eat them up and then struggle to stay awake, enjoying the madness before lining up another choof on the crack pipe.

It was becoming increasingly hard to evaluate the damage done the night before as I was going into blackouts even after the first drink, I would talk to people that weren't there and accuse Frank of cheating on me with the neighbor. No matter how long he took to explain his actions, I would think he was lying to me. If he went downstairs to the shop to buy cigarettes during one of our 5-day benders, I would lie prostrate on the floor, peering underneath our front door, listening for every sound, door opening, and bird chirp, feeling sure I was going to catch him in the act.

During our week-long party escapades, I would analyze the placement of the mugs and glasses on our kitchen table to make sure that, when I got back from the bathroom, nothing had moved and, if by chance anything had, I would accuse him of sleeping with the girl next door, feeling certain she had been in the apartment while I was on the loo.

I lay there weighing up the pros and cons of another debauch and pondered what my life would be like if I wasn't doing this. As far back as I could remember, I had always been the party girl. It was my way of connecting with people. It was what I thought I brought to friendships and what I admired in people around me. It was how I used to deal with pain. It was what I had built my whole identity on. Who would I be without it? I had no idea, but I knew one thing for sure, my spirit was sick and the little girl inside me was heartbroken over what I had become.

On that particular day, there was something inside that told me that if I kept going like this, I would surely die or go mad. The emptiness in my chest was like breathing broken glass, and for a moment, I had the first honest thought that I'd had in a very long time, maybe even ever. Staring at the ceiling, I said out loud:

Please, God, let me not drink or take any drugs today because I think I'm going to die.

The prayer was crystal clear. Never had I spoken to God, or thought that there was any sort of loving kindness there to look after me. Never.

Everything went silent. I waited there for a minute, teetering on the edge of a great fence. I caught a glimpse of myself in the mirrored wardrobe. It was upsetting to see myself like that and even more upsetting to know I was going to go straight out into that living room and poor myself a drink and have a line of coke. It was my first realization that I couldn't stop myself even though I wanted to. I was powerless. That prayer was the first sign to myself, and to any Higher Power, that I had, in fact, for the very first time, surrendered.

Our bed was low to the ground—a futon. This had long been helpful at times like this when getting out of bed was a bit of a struggle. I would drag myself to the edge of the mattress, trying my best to navigate my way past the dirty ashtrays and half-drunk beverages that I had placed on the wooden bed frame the night before. There would be a collection of them encircling our bed, and after knocking down the chardonnay and smoking the last coke cigarette, I would succumb to the hazy world of the Xanax that always concluded our prolonged debauches.

I steadied myself before attempting to stand up; my legs were like dead iron weights; my knees were jittery and unstable, and I felt sick to my stomach.

I grabbed for my hair elastic, thinking that putting my hair up might make me look more awake, and wandered into the bathroom to brush my teeth. Lord only knew how long it had been. Putting sweatpants on with one of Frank's hoodies, I did my best to look presentable and slowly opened the door and peered into the living room.

"Sez! You've finally woken up!" Frank said, as he continued puffing on his cigarette.

"How long have I been asleep?" I mumbled.

"Since yesterday morning. So probably about 30-something hours." Frank was concerned, but there were people there, so he didn't want to make too much of a fuss. He had been trying to get me to slow down for some time.

I walked as gracefully as I could into the kitchen, which overlooked the living room, making sure my feet were securely planted on the floor before putting my weight down. Hitting the deck while we had guests was not something I wanted to do. I surveyed the scene and evaluated what my chances were of convincing the guys to give me a line of coke. I thought if I appeared to be taking care of myself by making a couple of bags of 2-minute noodles, my chances would improve. Heating up 2-minute noodles was, in fact, the only thing I could do in the kitchen besides making a cheese single sandwich and pouring drinks. But even the latter was sometimes too overwhelming, depending on the amount of cocaine I had consumed and who was watching me from the living room. When I made 2-minute noodles, I always cooked them in a saucepan, which I thought made up for the fact that I couldn't actually cook and that this wasn't really cooking. It appeared like I was cooking pasta and felt like it, too. Of course, I was only fooling myself, and anyone who didn't get close enough to look in my pot.

Convincing everyone that I was good to go, and Frank, trying to avoid another argument, finally poured me a drink and I was off to the races again! I had no way of knowing at the time that he would end up being one of the first people to support me get clean and sober. He would be the one to hold my hand as I made that terrifying decision to surrender. At one of the most important crossroads of my life, he was there.

Partying through to the early hours the next day, I found myself all out of coke, Xanax, and alcohol. Frank was asleep and snoring and I was losing my friggin' mind. The harrowing loneliness and despair in the early hours of that morning were some of the worst moments I can recall. I hope I never forget them. Desperately wanting it all to stop but not knowing how, I organized more drugs, a driver, and a hostage to take with me to pick up the coke from the bar. But this time, it was different. It would be my last hurrah. The divine *had* heard the very first prayer I had ever said.

Reluctant as I was to follow any kind of spiritual path, I found myself surrendering to a program of recovery in August 2006 and began learning about personal responsibility, forgiveness, and healing. At that time, I was unaware of the impact of trauma and its many manifestations. The generational inheritance of emotional, mental, and spiritual malaise was not something I even knew I had. These toxic patterns had been instilled in my family through lifetimes of pain and suffering until they made their way to me. At the age of 27, I began to unpack and collapse these kingdoms once and for all.

The spiritual path is not a straight line. We grow in spirals. Sometimes we must hit something repeatedly until we have processed all of it. This may seem at times like we are going backwards, but my experience has shown me otherwise. Sometimes these wounds may never fully be repaired but will, in our pursuit of healing, take us on a remarkable journey of self-discovery and rich experience that will illuminate our soul and gift us with wisdom.

As I entered my first year of recovery, a dear friend suggested I try meditation. Being resistant to this suggestion, I declined many times until her persistence and nagging got the better of me and I caved.

You have to understand that I came from a life where drugs and alcohol were king, and the Underbelly of Australia was my family. My lifestyle was hard and fast-paced, and I lived my life in accordance with the rules of the Underworld. So, you can understand why meditation seemed a little flaky to me. I couldn't see how it would help the part of me who had needed to ingest kilos and liters of mind-altering substances just to get a hit! I mean, what effect could meditation really have?

Nevertheless, I followed my friend's suggestion and began attending groups at the local Shanti Mission Harmony Center in Sydney, NSW. (Even the name gave me the heebie-jeebies!) It was there that I met the teacher of the school, Shakti Durga, and began taking her classes.

One of the most memorable experiences I ever had—and there have been many—was when I engaged in a meditation class on forgiveness. Historically, I hated this word for a few reasons. I mean, did anyone ever *truly* forgive? I had heard a lot of lip service about forgiveness, much spiritual bypassing with people claiming to be spiritual giants by taking the higher road over their perpetrators, but *really?* I wasn't convinced. I also felt that forgiveness was a sign of weakness—that you were condoning the other person's behavior, and you were defeated. This was something I had fought against my whole life.

But again, I was trying to do things differently, so I engaged in the exercise anyway.

Shakti Durga told us to "pick someone in your life that you *really* struggle with. Someone with whom there has been a lot of pain and suffering." Well, that was easy. I would make my dad the focus of the meditation.

It had taken me 15 years to circle back around and even *consider* having a relationship with him. The connection had been severed when I was twelve, and I had held the burning rage of my childhood for so long that I wondered who I would be without it. It had been why I did all the stupid things in my life. But in that first year since entering recovery and learning about forgiveness, I reached out and connected with my dad.

The first conversation was awkward as we hadn't spoken for many years. He told me a story about a couple of birds that kept flying into his house and landing on his kitchen table. I knew he was trying to make a connection with me, and so I entertained his story about the white dove and pigeon, saying how crazy it was they were doing that. He loved all animals and had a very kind heart in that way. I think that was one of the reasons my mum had loved him. When I spoke to him another time that year, he told me again of the incoming birds. So up until this point, our connection had been entirely centered around a white dove and a pigeon.

Sitting in that forgiveness meditation, I knew I was at a crossroads. Did I want to heal, or did I want to keep the door open to my old lifestyle? The choice was ultimately mine to make.

I sat there with my eyes closed as Shakti Durga led us through a guided meditation. We chanted the sacred *Ho'oponopono* song, "I'm sorry, please forgive me, thank you, I love you," as tears rolled down my face. I remembered a time with my dad when I was so full of rage that I had spoken to someone about getting him taken out or "knocked," as we say in Australia. My 16-year-old mind thought the best way to fix the problem was to get rid of the person I thought was causing all the trouble, and then everyone would be okay. In my naivety, I had made it my mission to avenge the pain of my family. Thankfully I was caught, and nothing ever progressed. Years later, I was reminded of those feelings as I sat in the meditation. For the first time in my life, I felt the pain I had caused him with my own actions, and I wanted to make it right.

In the meditation, I could see us both sitting out on the back porch of the family home. I was singing to him, and he was singing to me, both of us owning our actions and yearning for forgiveness. Up until that point, I hadn't seen myself clearly. I had blamed my dad my whole life—for everything. I never saw the pain of his inner little boy. I never considered that he, too, had been abused and traumatized; I just blamed him for all of it. It was a profound moment of healing and understanding, and, in the meditation, sitting between us on the back porch was the white dove, which I perceived as a symbol of peace.

Shakti Durga eventually asked us to open our eyes and come back into our bodies. I was still crying and very much activated by all the energy in the meditation, but I slowly opened my eyes. It was one of my strongest experiences with meditation, and I was taken aback by its power. She explained that we were breaking for lunch and asked us to be back in an hour. I reached into my bag to check my phone before heading out and saw that I had one message. It was from my dad. When I opened the message, I saw, to my surprise, that he had sent me a photo of the white dove! He had sent it while I was focusing on him in the meditation. He didn't know I was doing that, of course, but his soul did!

In that moment, I understood the power of meditation and energy healing and what can happen when you work with another person on a soul level. They receive the healing without even needing to be there in the physical! It's all about energy and intention.

My relationship with my father began to heal after that meditation and it has continued over the years. It has been a journey of forgiveness, compassion, letting go of expectations and everything in between. I feel so blessed to do this work alongside so many other courageous trailblazers. it blows my mind every day!

Surrounded by swooping Oak and Olive trees, I hear the joyful chirping of neighborhood birds. The sun is shining through our glass sliding doors as it hits a six-pointed glass prism, sending multiple little rainbows of light across the room. Butchananda, my little Lhasa Apso, is quietly sleeping at the distinguished age of 16 years and nine months old, and I am filled to the brim with a deep sense of gratitude. I share my space at the Narayani ashram with two other devotees and enjoy a life of service and devotion. It has already been an incredible journey, and I am only 16 years and 8 months sober.

The foundation of my life today is service, devotion, and healing. I have experienced many mystical experiences that surpass the rational mind and have no real explanation other than divine grace. I founded a charity called "The Brahman Project Foundation," a humanitarian organization focused on spiritual education, prison rehabilitation, and animal welfare. Sri Sakthi Amma is my Guru, the living embodiment of Divine Mother and great Avatar of our time. I lead her Narayani Center spiritual community here in San Diego, California, where we engage in devotional practices that help connect us with the divine. Half my week is spent serving the population at Donovan State Prison with our "Freedom on the Inside Prison Project." We teach trauma-informed healing, mantra, and meditation, and create conscious programming such as Restorative Justice Fairs, Mural Projects, Tattoo Removal Programs, Carnivals, and Days of Recovery. My heart will be forever closely connected to this population, as I believe it was only by divine luck that I managed to escape incarceration myself, all those years ago.

I have dived into the darkest places within myself and brought it all up to heal, reclaiming the little girl within, and all the parts of me that were lost in separateness, shame, and trauma. I have needed help along the way, and I still do. This life has not been a tidy one. It has been messy and painful, brilliant, and miraculous, and I wouldn't miss a single second of it. If I could go back and speak to the scared 27-year-old girl who thought she wouldn't be able to live without drugs or alcohol for even one day, it would be to tell her that she is stronger than she knows and the Divine has got her every step of the way.

Om Namo Narayani

BRAHMANKYRIE

BrahmanKyrie is a spiritual leader, teacher, and energy healer who lives in Encinitas, California. She is the founder of "The Brahman Project," a humanitarian foundation focused on spiritual education for the soul, sacred ceremonies, meditation, healing, prison rehabilitation programs, and support for animals both in the USA and globally.

BrahmanKyrie has also created "Freedom on the Inside Prison Project," offering Restorative Justice Fairs, Mural Projects, and Tattoo Removal Programs. She is completely devoted to serving her community in the temple and in the prison.

BrahmanKyrie weaves trauma-informed Inner-child healing with ancient Sanskrit mantras to liberate her clients from past traumas and blockages. Her wisdom teachings, coupled with emotional mastery, are potent platforms for self-realization, personal empowerment, and attaining deep peace.

Om Namo Narayani

www.thebrahmanproject.com
www.freedomontheinside.org

FREE GIFT

Zoom Inner Child Healing Session

In this session, you will connect with your inner child and experience healing and transformation.

To schedule, visit **www.thebrahmanproject.com**

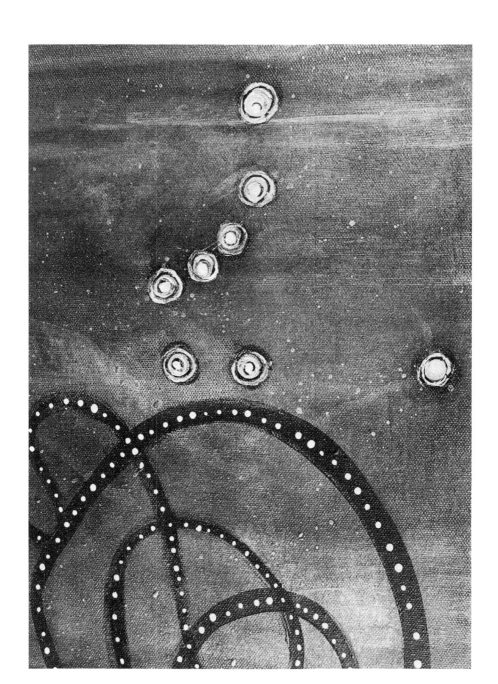

CHAPTER 7

If I Do Not Speak, I Cannot Hear My Voice

By Sarah Devereux

The Welsh slang for microwave is *Popty Ping*—it makes me smile as I roll it around my mouth and mind. It's satisfying—*Popty Ping* and it is cooked. I was brought up with typewriters and I watched my mother type at her jobs, on the rare times she took me along. The end of a paragraph. *Tap, tap, tap, tap, ping.* The carriage return lever gets flung over. *Ping.* I always thought I would use a typewriter. I think I knew that I always wanted to write and that there would be a *ping* for my new paragraphs and end of sentences.

Now my life is punctuated by *pings* from machines and screens and phones. *Popty Ping*—the microwave that heats up the tea I abandoned, chasing a thought or a dream, or sitting with someone, untangling and understanding their story. *Popty Ping.* Imprints and wounds and compassion. It's the story of therapy. It's the sorting and shifting. It's a kaleidoscope, I say, and sometimes, it's mud. Sometimes the light floods through. More tea. *Popty Ping.*

The thing I don't want anyone to know is that I am scared to shine my light. The thing I don't want you to know is that when someone says the word *authentic* I shudder inside. I want you to be authentic, but I cannot give that space to myself.

I can steal a good story. The structure of this story I stole, like a magpie with a shiny precious jewel, from *Moon Tiger,* by Penelope Lively (Penguin,

1987). This book is/was a turning point—there is no straight line and if you want to know me, it's the strata of my life and you must excavate with me until we reach the core. We will circle round; we will return to the same place but with new perspectives as we understand the ground rock beneath.

I notice, as I write these words, that I feel shame that I cannot write in a straight line. When I was little, they encouraged me to write on lined paper because I always veered off the page. I suspect that veering off the page is where the magic is!

I was 34 and I went to a solar eclipse camp and I came back and I stared at the toast on the grill. My then-husband made a comment about what I had been up to, and I realised that I should leave and I didn't. Turning point missed.

In Welsh, microwaves are called *Popty Ping,* and I feel like my life has been dominated, more or less, by the *Popty Ping* of a microwave. He left me, having fallen in love with someone else, and I blamed him but I never said, in authenticity, I wanted to leave. I left first—I just didn't pack my bags. I hid out in my own life.

I am 32 when someone close accuses me of not supporting them, and I crumble inside. *Popty Ping.* I don't want to do that again.

I am 50 and I am working and working and working, and we are still not making any money. We are still not making any money. *Popty Ping.* We owe a lot of money and *Popty Ping,* on a penny, I negotiate payment plans, interest suspension, and reasonable payments. I am scared. Turning point missed.

I am 3 and I want to leave home. *Popty Ping.* I am 9 and I leave home. *Popty Ping.* It just didn't feel right. I want back because I don't have anywhere to go. I am 10 and I go to tea in someone else's house and this time, I don't go home for about 40 years. *Popty Ping.*

Popty Ping. Where do we hide out and where do we claim space for ourselves?

"The problem with you is that you will always do what you want to do," they say. *Popty Ping.* "What's the problem with that?" I think. "Shouldn't you always do what you want to do?" I look at life differently from other people and realise that I have an 'odd view.' Mick Dervla is a bad boy in my class. Mick Dervla has always been bad—in the same way that Gina was always black—don't say black, say coloured—always. *Popty Ping* of the casually horrific racism and of a Catholic schooling in West London in the '70s. Here it was "pull up the ladder," if you were Irish or Portuguese or Spanish, *Popty Ping.* If you were Grenadian or Jamaican, not *Popty Ping*—even though we went to the same church, we did not drink in the same clubs or bars. Same God, different bars, *Popty Ping.*

Mick Dervla got expelled at age 12 because he threw a knife at the teacher. *Popty Ping.* Mick Dervla got expelled because the teaching staff were tired of him. He was getting taller and they saw a golden opportunity when Mick lobbed a school dinner knife across the room and it sailed over the head of Mrs. Rock as she walked—late again—into the room. Everyone knew that school dinner cutlery couldn't cut paper and that he hadn't thrown it at Mrs Rock. Mick Dervla was expelled for throwing a knife at a teacher and I know there was a different story. I didn't know I could even tell a different story.

I just kept the different stories inside me—Popty Ping.

I am 5 and I am in charge of a brigade of soldiers. I make them march down the road with me and back up again. I march them a lot, every day. I am in charge of them. I march them a lot. My mum is impatient while I walk up and down the slope a lot, as she wants to get home. It's a big house and I don't like to go to sleep. *Popty Ping.* I hold onto my mother's finger every night. She does not hold me. I tell the story of her dedication in holding my finger. I did not tell the story that she never liked to hold me. *Popty Ping.*

I am 7 and I have made my first Holy Communion and then I take my dress off and go to North End Road market for veg with my mum. I like my dress. It's a big day. The story I tell myself is that in the 70s, they did not give parties for kids for Holy Communion. *Popty Ping.* They did. Just not for me.

I go to the theatre and watch the pantomime and it is so beautiful. I go to dancing school and dance and sing and act. I am alive and scared because it's strict and hard work. It's beautiful.

I am 57 and I realise when I am asked to write something, that it will be about how I am in the world, and I feel dizzy and nauseous. I will have to ground myself. I will have to write from what I know. I will have to write from authenticity. I feel sick and put my head between my legs. Not *Popty Ping.*

I am 12 and I am so in love. He is Italian and beautiful and I cannot hide it. He is 16 and not in love with me. I do not understand why you have to hide this amazing feeling. I am teased a lot. He is a fourth year and I am a first year. I learn this story the hard way. I am odd. I speak posh and I act strangely, and I am not interested in things that other girls are and I don't give a shit about what others think. *Popty Ping.* But then this burns and shames, and maybe they are right, there is something wrong with me...Not *Popty Ping.* My love lasts for two years and I am always in the wrong story. I work in the library and he rules the playground.

Popty Ping. I don't like the story and I don't get it. I am allowed to kiss a boy, but only once, and only one at time, and then they have to walk you home. I get drunk on Gaymer's Olde English Cider and kiss three boys and walk myself home. One boy tells me that he is angry with me because I kissed another boy. I am confused. One girl gets mad at me because I tell my friend she is wearing false nails. I think it's funny. I am confused. Not *Popty Ping.*

I am 22 and I read a book that says there is no linear progression in our lives only—stories are layered and to reveal ourselves, someone must be prepared to excavate. *Popty Ping.* This is me.

My story is always end, middle, and sometimes, beginning. Always repeating. I insist on reading the end of books all the time. I want a trowel to start excavating but most people want beginning, middle, and end, it seems.

I will always do what I want to do. Will I? I go to the theatre and watch the pantomime and it is so amazing. Peach pink lights and girls dancing. It is beautiful. I discover plays and scripts—stories, glorious stories which behave themselves. They do what they say they will. I say my lines. You say your lines, and IT NEVER CHANGES. Add lights and people who love it when these stories are told, and I AM HOME. I want to live in the theatre. So, I do. Nobody notices that I am in three different plays and fail nine O-levels and then can't do A-levels. I want to do theatre badly. It is the place where my heart sings. But there are different stories that I don't want to see. Dad hates the pantos, the dances, and the suitcases full of costumes. This is the story. The car is broken into. The window is broken. My lovely vanity case stolen. Tap shoes gone. The window is worth more than the car, he says. My story is my tears for my beautiful case. *Popty Ping.*

He is so beautiful, and 17. I cannot believe how beautiful he is, and that he loves me. I belong. He is intense. I don't do A-levels, I do him. Who gives a fuck about university? I am sick and vomiting and 18. I am so tired and selling children's shoes. I am pregnant. I am wearing my green overalls. I am so tired one day, that I sit on the top step and say, "I am sorry." I can't work much harder, I am pregnant. *Popty Ping. Popty Ping. Popty Ping.*

Popty Ping. I am so scared. And he is so beautiful. The top of his head is so beautiful. My heart pumps and aches. 31 years later, I hold his son and smell the top of his head and the story continues. Ma. Then Grandma.

I am 7 and Dad tells me about the mysteries, and that you think about them when you say the rosary. You need to know the decades of the rosary when you make your First Holy Communion. It's not all about the dress—isn't it? I swallow the bread and it sticks to the roof of my mouth. Nothing happens. Lots of *pop* but no *ping*. Twenty years later, the nun in the church—there is always one of the sisters attached to the church—asks if there can be a limit set on the amount of money (read, hundreds of pounds) and frills spent on Holy Communion Dresses and warfare is declared. Did she not realise in the immigrant communities that this is God in action?

I sit in a Quaker meeting house in Yorkshire and the silence envelops me—this is not my God, but I like the silence and they always serve tea and biscuits afterwards. The silence swirls around me—comforting, cheerful, and undemanding. I find the talking time more challenging. During the silence this Sunday, I hear the voice of a young girl, as her mother gently tells her to be quiet...and in the silence, the little girl says, "If I do not speak, I cannot hear my voice." This resonates in my head like the loudest gong ever. Of course. I rush out and scribble the words down on a piece of paper. It is in my bathroom to this day.

If I do not speak, I cannot hear my voice.

Every day, I have a bath and I think about how to sound my voice. I float, blow bubbles, and deliberate.

How is my voice foregrounded—how do I make my voice known? In the core of the strata, what is the story that I need to tell? How do I tell my story, and how do I find the words to tell it? Why do I need to tell my story? The words have always tumbled out, but will anyone connect with what I am saying in my darker moments? I wonder why I must write and speak. And then the light comes again, morning comes, and I know that I write to connect. I write to attach. I write to come into connection with you. I write to find the common ground where we can meet.

The temple and my sister invite my voice and my story and, initially, I don't trust it. I understand the internal censor that has very successfully done the job of the Catholic—not Greek—chorus...mainly of guilt and condemnation. Great Mother tells me, "All of you is completely welcome here," and I realise that I cannot tolerate that. It takes me several years to accept the true nature of that love and invitation for my voice. The initiation is clear—your voice without shame. The initiation is powerful. The first time I address a Zoom room with 300 beings, my laptop crashes and I have to come back in and hold space without guilt or shame but with resonance and authenticity.

My work as a therapist has always been about where the voices are and where the stories are. In *All's Well That Ends Well*, Shakespeare says, "The web of our life is a mingled yarn, good and ill together…" It is in this mingled yarn that I have found my greatest stories. In relationships, where my voice is heard and appreciated. Appreciation is such an outdated concept, it seems, but for me, it is a combination of love and savouring that I find very pleasing.

What am I thinking about when writing for this book? I come across the term 'foreground' by Foulkes. In terms of foreground in group analysis, it is the concept of how the position of the individual and group are related by context, with the individual in the foreground and the group in the background, but the meaning is determined by the context of the whole.

It is in this meaning that I understand my journey, which has been to foreground my voice in spite of, supported by, or challenged by the context of the group in the background and its power over my voice.

I suspect in my life I have always had an eye to the group in the background and what they have wanted me to say. I feel in my body the stretch towards my desire and the constraint of expectation, that is now so internalised that it does not have to be embodied.

I think that our present-day witch wound is co-dependence. It is the word that takes a lot of space in our milieu. My thinking is that the quality of the voice that is foregrounded and is different from the group, is that of the other…the witch, the priestess, the person of magic, transformation, non-gendered. I think when we play small or conciliatory, we activate the place which, trans-generationally, has been where we need to shut up because it's not safe to speak or think.

It is not surprising to me, in my body, how strong the pull is to be considered allied to someone else's desires. If I really told you my deepest desires, you would at the very least unfriend me or ghost me. I think this is our contemporary version of being silenced, murdered, tortured, or cancelled. For those voices in other physical spaces in the world who are other, silencing, torture, and violence are still all too present.

Popty Ping. We teach our children well to push down those powerful voices of desire and inquiry. When I think about the reason to write, it is to free and model an uncensored voice. It is to feel in my body the echo of my voice and my truth. This is a work in progress. In this, I feel the essence of connections informed by good boundaries and healthy desires.

Popty Ping—Addendum

I love the word *Addendum*. I am not even sure I know what it means. It just feels right. *Addendum*. It's like another version of *Popty Ping*. The end with a bit added on. *Addendum*. The bit added on. I like it. My bit added on is this. I was so excited about the editing process for this chapter. I AM GOING TO BE EDITED. It felt magnificent. Then I was edited and... *something*. A blur that I could not quite put my finger on and that whisked out of view every time, I turned my head to catch it.

What is it? I feel dizzy and disorientated. *Addendum. Addendum.* What is the bit that is disappearing around the corner? It's a fuss-making bit. It's a flipperty gibbet—worst insult in my English nan's world. Closely followed by those who make a 'fuss.' I AM MAKING A FUSS. The editing process feels like someone has taken my voice, I think.

There I have said it—I have made a fuss.

Then the scales fall from my eyes. I realise that I have been so taken with my voice in my head that I have become insular. Like Narcissus, I have fallen in love with the beauty of my own reflection. I also avoid the vulnerable-making bit—you might not like what I say, so let me keep it in my head. Let me keep myself from your gaze.

Then I realise what editing is and it reminds me that my writing is no more mine than that blade of grass, outside my window. My writing is mine and yours and ours. I believe it probably comes in expression from 'her upstairs' but whatever floats your boat.

It is the culmination of all the voices I have listened to and spoken with and dreamed with and whose worlds have entwined with and I have ventured into.

I realise that your voices and the editors of this chapter are part of the long exposure that brings this chapter into being—into a complex, layered form. In the 1800s, a photograph could take an hour to expose. In a landscape photograph, people, animals, and weather would have passed through in that time but never be recorded in the final image. I like to think that there is a record in the final composition, of your presence and my presence. In their very essence and the feeling evoked by the—not my words, we are all there.

Are we not all changed by connection and contact? I am changed in every moment—it's in the exposure for the photo, the image you may never see but always feel. It's the figure that was never exposed but is as vital in its presence to the photo as any other part of the composition. In that moment of exposure, we are connected. I will see you and you will be in my writing forever. My voice will entwine with yours and say it out loud—"If I do not speak, I cannot hear my voice. I cannot hear your voice."

SARAH DEVEREUX

I have worked in mental health services in the public sector for the past twenty-five years. I am a psychotherapist, passionate about the process of change through the reclamation of our story and in the validation, its ability to support everyone in living the life that they wish to live. I delight in supporting people in finding the space and strength to gain clarity around patterns of relating and ways of behaving, which may no longer serve them. I have been known to throw everything in the air from time to time and 4 years ago moved from London, my home and comfort zone to Hereford, 1/2 mile down a single-track lane. I am meditating on, enquiring in, and now writing about the new iteration of the witch at the end of the lane or, more likely, the priestess at the end of the path. I am as ever supported by the love of the Priestess Presence temple and initiation and sisterhood in Enter the Mystery circle. To the one heart.

Learn more at **sarahdevereuxuk.ddns.net**

An audio file of Sarah reading her Turning Point chapter, "If I Do Not Speak, I Cannot Hear My Voice."

If you enjoyed my story, or if you prefer listening to books (which I do, as I love being read to), I am pleased to be able to give you a recording of me reading my story.

So grab a cup of team and please visit my webpage **sarahdevereuxuk.ddns.net** where I read this story aloud.

CHAPTER 8

The Party's Over: Welcome Back to Earth School

By Caryl Anne Engel

It was the Spring of 1975, and my high school drama club had just wrapped our show *Li'l Abner,* which included the Broadway classic song, *It's a Typical Day in Dog Patch USA!* At age 15, I was in love with the stage, *and* with gooney-eyed Paul Brenkus. I was in heaven.

One of our song numbers was *Sadie Hawkins Day Dance*—that wacky reverse love-fest, where girls got to chase the boys one day of the year. The same night the show wrapped, Laura Rosen hosted the cast party in her dimly lit living room.

Would this be *my* Sadie Hawkins Day chance? Could I finally tell Paul I loved him? Paul had lips the color of salmon, and I had longed to kiss them since 10th grade. He was now a senior. Was I seeing signs that he liked me, too?

I followed him into the den as the record player played. This was my moment. I bravely sat beside him and stammered with a mouth full of Fritos, "Do ya' wan-some? Were you glad you were in *Li'l Abner?*"

We joked about our director, Mr. Barner's childish temper tantrums, and our song numbers.

"I really enjoyed being in the show with you, Caryl," Paul said.

What? Really? My heart skipped a beat but no words came out.

Paul moved closer and rested his hand next to mine. I was sure I really was in heaven, soaring, when he leaned in and moved his lips close to my face...

Suddenly, my teenage radar was on red alert. Out of the corner of my eye, I could see *an adult!* Why, oh why, was Laura Rosen's FATHER in the room?

It soon became crystal clear that Laura's wicked sense of humor was inherited. Mr. Rosen was on a mission...a lethal one! Slinking over to the record player, he slowly pulled a black LP out of its jacket and replaced David Bowie's "Changes" on the turntable with a new record. He carefully selected the track, whispering, "Okay, kids, listen up."

Nat King Cole's voice began to croon...

The Party's Over...Time to call it a day. You always knew it would end this way...The party's over...Over my friend.

Then Mr. Rosen simply said, "Hate to kill a good time, kids. Time to clear out! Tennis in the morning. Sorry."

Sorry? I turned to Laura with a desperate look, "Can't you *do* something?"

I heard several snickers...theater kids appreciate this kind of humor. Another kid mumbled, "But Mr. Rosen, it's our cast party!" Another kid just resignedly sighed and said, "Bummer."

Over. Just. Like. That.

The degree to which adults can kill a good time, with criminal detachment and zero remorse, is staggering.

Paul shifted over, rubbing his eyes. "I guess we have to clear out," he said.

"Wher' you wanna go, Paul? Another party?" I stammered desperately.

"I have to work tomorrow," he said. "It was really fun being in the musical with you, Caryl." He looked down at his lap, and then up at me, blushing. And then, of all the strange teenage boy things to do, he picked up my hand and kissed it, holding his lips there for a moment.

He sighed again, and said, "I wish we could have...you know..."

I looked down and blushed, and in the first fully formed sentence of our communication, I said softly, "I know Paul. I like you, too."

Then he said the last words I would ever hear from his lips:

"Hey Andy, can you give me a ride home?"

I choked down sobs in Laura's downstairs half-bathroom.

Paul's a senior and is not coming back next year. Lil Abner's over, too.

Worst of all, I had to call my mother to pick me up. I sucked my 38F Sophia Loren-sized love back into my mosquito-bitten chest to hold my broken heart.

Laura's dad, Mr. Rosen, had just earned the "Lifetime MVP Every Party Has a Pooper" Award.

"But Paul does love me, I think! Maybe there's a chance!" I looked down at my hand and vowed that I would *never, ever* wash it, as passion coursed through my body.

Once I got home, my mother offered me a bowl of Goldfish crackers. I studied her as I munched them. My mother has a lush Venus-like figure. And there's my dark, curvy, seductress sister who wore Egyptian Eye Makeup (as my dad calls it.)

What happened to me? Answer: My oldest sister and I inherited our father's physique—tall, lean, and spare. She later moved to a spiritual commune. Breastfeeding her new baby, she would say, with feminist defiance: "Now, Caryl, this is what women's breasts are really for!" And I would look at her and think, "Wrong. Women's breasts are for shoving into tight sweaters with cleavage so that they can allure men. They're to bust out of skimpy bathing suit tops—and in case you haven't noticed, we are totally screwed in this area this lifetime."

Sigh. The long depressing summer stretched before me, with no chance of ever seeing Paul Brenkus again.

But WAIT! Maybe there was a way!

I devised a plan and got my friend Lisa to ride bikes past his house, just pretending to 'be in the neighborhood.' We casually chatted for about 45 minutes in his driveway, until his mother came out asking concernedly, "Can I *help* you, girls?" After which humiliation, we made the long, pathetic, teenage bike ride home.

Now, as an adult, I understand that throughout our lives we suffer so many little deaths, like the end of a great show, or our summer vacation coming to a close. Losses big, losses small.

But please entertain me for a moment: Isn't that *just like* the Soul? The Soul has places to go and people to meet. The Soul says, "Hate to kill a good time, but YOU, Little Missy, are marching straight to bed because you need a good night's sleep! You've got a *biiiiiiig* Lifetime coming up tomorrow! Oh, please, dear. Stop whining. You signed up for this, remember?"

So many times during my own life initiations, I found myself thinking, "No, I do not remember signing up for Earth School. I don't buy that heaven stuff, and I did NOT come here to learn big life lessons. I'm just fine, thank you."

Hmm.

There was an *Oprah* show with a (formerly skeptical) surgeon, Eben Alexander, who wrote the *New York Times* bestseller, *Proof of Heaven*, about his near-death experience. If you didn't read it, he reports back that "heaven is for real."

Many others who've had near-death experiences say heaven—The Other Side, Way Up There, or whatever you want to call it—is like a Renaissance painting on steroids...so mind-bendingly beautiful and peaceful, entertaining, and full of wisdom and fun that you never want to come back. Folks who've crossed over after an accident or medical incident seem to be, at first, universally bummed about being sucked back into their broken Earth School body. In heaven, everything is joyful and illuminated.

And then, BOOM, ouch, pain meds! More life to live. Yet, they sport a calm smile more often and exude a knowing, *Now, I remember now why I came—I have a purpose! There's more to life than it appears. Isn't that wonderful?*

Each time we choose to reincarnate back here, in Earth School, it must feel like the close of a great show or the abrupt end of a beautiful party.

Huh? Wha' just happened? Mr. Rosen!

No matter how great the family you were karmically assigned to or how many opportunities life provides you with, there are still painful crushes. But heaven, by all reports, is like your best day on Earth…times one million. With better weather. And no one is ever in a bad mood. Particularly you.

Imagine that each time you come back to Earth, your Soul cheerfully announces, "It's going to be an amazing life, kiddo! Sure, maybe a few, uh, 'snafus' here and there. Nothing you can't handle!"

You roll your eyes. You've heard this line before.

If your Soul is anything like mine, it's been down here *many* times. And without fail, each time, it says snarkily, in that eternal teenage-to-parent communication style: "Oh *thanks*, Soul, you with your Big Plans. You suck, by the way. I just love how you say, 'You just need to clear a bit of karmic debt!' or, 'Poverty builds character!' or, 'Sorry, you'll be 4 feet tall this time— but look at those big baby blue eyes!' Oh yes, I love it when you tell me, 'Smallpox develops character. Next time you'll come back as a great doctor!'"

For sure, there are those Souls who barrel down the birth canal like kids headed for Ft. Lauderdale on Spring Break, ready for the party of a lifetime. Woo-Hoo! Me? I held onto the womb walls in a death grip. This time I had to be induced, two weeks late, chanting that Vietnam War peace chant, "Hell, no, I won't go!" I've had my foot on the brakes half this life already.

Now to be sure, most folks sign up for a few rigorous classes, at least in one area or another. Sometimes *my* life has felt like an ongoing AP class. I wonder, do spiritual teachers and writers sign up for bigger course loads, so they can report what they learned to others?

Yes, I think so.

Spirit has a great sense of humor.

As I'm writing this in Starbucks, I hear coming over the music sound system: "*Don't want to die anymore; it's a long road home….*" And next, Johnny Cash's "Burn Burn Burn, the Ring of Fire."

Two of my Spirit Guides, Hanlon and Gabriella, are in the car driving me back to Earth School. It would take 45 Earth years for me to remember who they were and to say hello! (If being a Spirit Guide isn't a thankless job, I don't know what is…these two have put up with me for centuries; bless THEIR souls. So, let's celebrate *Thank Your Guides* week, and take them somewhere nice, like the Astral Luncheonette!)

"Now, dear," they say, like parents being patient with their emotionally disturbed teenage daughter, "Don't you remember those nice tour brochures we pored over? Remember the lovely countries you'd visit this lifetime? France and Italy? And those nice people from the 13th century you'll get to see again?"

"Please, I just want to stay HOME with YOU!" I cry.

They shake their heads. I must go through with it. My new mother's name is Peggy, and she is pregnant. There's my Soul's contract to fulfill.

"Your nice friend Lisa is coming! You'll meet her in 6th grade and have the exact same sense of humor. And your friend Beth, well, there's that little incident in Washington, DC, in 7th grade, which will pretty much ruin the next 6 years of your life, but…" (Gabriella shoots Hanlon a look to ZIP IT!) "Oh, yes…look for your funny friend Bob. And Wendy—she always knows when to call. You'll meet as toddlers and remain friends throughout your lives. Your middle sister is so funny—she'll get you through life's worst predicaments. And you will learn a lot from your strong, successful older sister."

Gabriella continues, "At age 10, you'll be able to walk into a room and feel other people's pain. You are wiser than many adults, but no one listens to you. You will feel sad. No one sees your grief. It will make you a very good actress. Also, you'll find two ticks in your crotch after hiking in the Rocky Mountains, but don't worry, you'll get them out."

I feel like I have bad travel guides.

"Look, you're going to the Amazon! And if you don't get bitten by the deadly poisonous snakes, you'll have a *grand t*ime! Look at those Toucans!"

I am now engulfed in sobs. "Whose shitty idea WAS it anyway, to come back to Earth School?"

They close their eyes and shake their heads, sighing, each and every time, as they must repeat: "*Yours, dear.*"

"Oh yes, and one last important tidbit: when you go back, you will develop amnesia, and totally forget this conversation ever happened."

"Huh?" I ask.

"Well, most folks never remember, dear. They blame their life on something else. But some humans want to find the answers to Earth School. They will try to learn life's larger lessons, and in particular, how they chose their lifetime. That's how the Soul evolves. We will amuse ourselves with heavenly activities until you remember we're here to continue this conversation."

"Can't I just be in a high school musical forever?" I ask them.

They say nothing. I'm quiet. I'm beginning to feel all my 1500 years. No wonder I'm tired.

It's almost time to go. I look down and see the snowy winter evening of my new Midwestern home. There's a man with dark hair and a woman with fine features at the dinner table. They're my new mother and father. They have two little girls, 5 and 7, my guides say. The younger one favors her father. I smile; she looks like a little gypsy. The mother says something, and the little girl jumps up and yells, "Yippee! A new baby!" The other sister seems concerned. I feel there's something else in the air...is it worry? As if they're wondering, *Is there enough to go around?*

Around me is Heaven's constant pastel twilight sky. I breathe in its eternal beauty. Indeed, my Guides say that each evening's twilight will be a gift, a reminder of home, that all is really well—and please, for Heaven's sake, lighten up. Friends now come to say goodbye. We'll see each other soon. Then a guy who's always making me laugh says, "Hey...look for me in high school. We'll be in a musical that has a weird name. Oh, and by the way.... I'll like you." And with a stage-like-pretend flourish of his hat, he kisses my hand.

I will return back here in the blink of an eye, but on Earth, that will feel like a very long time.

"Ready, dear?" I nod and close my eyes. I draw in the last scented breath of heaven...

The party's over...I always knew it would end this way.

CARYL ANNE ENGEL

Caryl's passion is using her voice and life experience, with humor, to help others heal. Caryl's gift is elucidating the Soul's path in shaping our life story. She has been on a lifelong journey to understand this phenomenon. Her joy is sharing this wisdom with her readers.

Caryl is Executive Assistant to the Publisher/CEO at Flower of Life Press and manages the bestselling **Turning Point** series of anthologies.

Caryl's spiritual counseling practice is Angel Speak. She communicates with Angels and discerns the Soul purpose of her clients as it relates to their gifts, talents, and life themes. Numerology, mediumship work, and past life readings guide her sessions. For Caryl, writing books and public speaking on these topics has become her life mission.

When not writing and speaking, Caryl enjoys hiking in nature, photography, creating mosaics, gardening, and traveling to sacred sites around the world. Her happy place is in the kitchen baking pies, yet she still misses summer thunderstorms off Lake Erie from her childhood. Caryl learned early on that cultivating a sense of humor will get you through just about anything in life.

Her book, *Girl Remembered—A Memoir* will be released in 2023.

Learn more at **girlremembered.com**

A chapter called, "Springbank Vision" from my upcoming book *Girl Remembered, a Memoir* (releasing in 2023).

In 2013, I began writing my memoir at Springbank Retreat Center in South Carolina. One night in bed, unable to sleep, I was visited by a large angel who guided me on an illuminating tour. It was a vision. Later, I realized I'd visited the Akashic Records (the Soul's Library of Congress!) where I was told much more about my life purpose and things to come.

To access your gift, visit **girlremembered.com.**

CHAPTER 9

In 1986, I Thought That I Had Found My Life...

By LaurenRose EveningSong

A Garden Of Awakening

I'm awakening.
Is it time?
Is it the best place?
How do we proceed?
Blessèd Be-ed us!
Blessèd Be-ed.
I've planted all these seeds
And there are some sprouting about;
Some are in the phase of gestating;
Some are in dormancy, waiting...
Here am I,
A garden of intention: connecting, transforming, and integrating.

It's really a mixture of things,
All 'sown' together.
Ah, little jokes, folks,
And we are on our way.

Writing is an occupation,
It occupies time AND space,
Intent, and place.
Writing in the Garden of my Awakening.
I open my eyes
To the Sun in the sky.
I see with hope;
I breathe, one with hope.
Emily Dickinson got it right:
Hope perches on the Heart,
Ready to fly into fullness.
A meter of a moment and time rushes,
Dances,
Flies forth.

What am I worth?
What are you worth?
We are Beings of Light
Intentionally set down in the Garden to open our eyes and see...
Set down into the Garden to open our ears and listen,
To deeply consider what we hear...
I CHALLENGE YOU ALL!
Can you awaken?
Can you open your eyes?
Your ears?
Your Heart?
Can you even start?
Then your mind will follow in kind.
Let it all begin.
Let it open at the opening.
"Let's dance!" Says my Vavnik Rabbi Friend.
"Let's spread Love audaciously."
"Let's include EVERYBODY!"
Yes.

She ventures a refrain:
"AUDACIOUSLY SPREADING ETERNAL UNCONDITIONAL LOVE,"
At the end of every email.
Yes.
Lets zip-on to her side of things, which is—all sides—for every soul!
Every Being!
'Cause we are all in this together, this Thing called "Living."
We are beings of Life.
We are Beings of Light.
We are Beings of Love.
Unconditionally.
What's that?
Letting 'weeds' grow in my Garden of Awakening…?
Hey wait! Who decides such a thing?
A weed is termed a useless plant, but…
There are no 'useless' plants,
No 'useless' insects,
No 'useless' ANYTHING in Creation.
There are no weeds.
Everything has a purpose,
Every plant—an intention.
Every animal—an intention.
Every Being—an Intention…!

Calling in Ann!
Y'all remember Ann?
Let me hear you;
Talk to me!
Inspire me some, Ann.
We are in A Garden of Awakening.
It is time.
A Garden! A Garden! We are in a Garden!

You see, I need your understanding, and perhaps your help.
How can I write if I don't have a theme?
How can I write if I don't have a word?
How can I sing if I don't have a note?
If I have a voice—it would wobble and dart,
Wobble and descend,
Wobble and ascend.
She replies:
 "Or, in varying fluctuations,
Beat a rhythm and dance its own rhyme."

Thank you Ann.
You heard me.
You see, they write through me.
So be it.

In 1986, I thought that I had found my life.

I was just 26 years old. However, it was not the case that I had found IT! But I had found Paris, France. I had found B, who led me to all of this. Yet, Paris was too urbane and just an emotional desert for me. It was a total spiritual blackout. *Oh, Mais oui!* (Oh, But yes!) right here in the "City of Lights." I was floundering in a milieu that was foreign not only because of culture and language; the Parisians were ambitious yet very closed emotionally and very materialistic, as of my initial experiences and very first impressions. As far as I could ascertain as a people—they possessed very little soul. When I first came to Paris, the people I met were hellbent on getting ahead of everyone else; there was so much stress and fear. They wore proverbial blinders. I would see them as urban lemmings, hordes of panicking animals concerned with only their careers and appearance; clothes, makeup, hair, perfumes, and *cigarettes*, jostling for their place at the traffic light in their cars or in line at the grocery store, métro, bus, or post office. *Dépêchez-vous! Dépêchez-vous!* (Hurry up! Hurry up!) The feeling of the place was dry, bitter, and very dark. Everyone seemed on the defensive and suspicious of each other. They criticized everyone and everything. I was a soulful American lost in an urbane desert of opposing values.

I had come from a soulful city of about medium size. Home was bright with sunshine, a lush green jungle hung with the Spanish Moss of *saveurs Créoles* (creole flavors), sights, smells, and sounds. Born as *La Nouvelle Orléans,* my birthplace was later baptized by the United States as "New Orleans; Southern Lady *extraordinaire."* She sang and sauntered slowly and soulfully on the Mighty Mississippi River. Yet, I left Her and went looking for the French roots of my home and my maternal ancestry. I had grown up in the suburban town of Chalmette, situated downriver from the city of New Orleans. Often when growing up, I was misconstrued by others or made fun of. I was a very sensitive child and wept easily. Then, added to my sensitivity, my interests were different than average. Perhaps it was because I understood or felt things beyond my ken. (And/or, as later understood, I empathically and unconsciously absorbed others' energies.) After attending the University of New Orleans (UNO) for a B.A. in Fine Arts and a Minor in Foreign Languages, I moved out of my parent's house and into the city proper. There I met this handsome and kind Frenchman, B., while I was living on Frenchmen Street in Le Faubourg Marigny, a neighborhood outside of the French Quarter. I was working nearby in a French Quarter art gallery at the time. B. was so positive and straightforward. I became intrigued and charmed by this man. When he had to return to France, I then visited Paris in the cold winter of 1985/86, became engaged in the spring, and we married that summer.

Oh! But what a shock!

At first, I tried to run with the lemmings; that is, tried to adapt and fit in. I continued with French courses where my American university study had left off. Then I tried my hand at Graduate Studies for a *License* (first year of Master's) in Art History at La Sorbonne/University of Paris IV. I got through the year but bombed the final exam. This wasn't my usual experience, bombing exams. Obviously, my academic French wasn't enough. Somewhere during all of this, I also worked at a foreign language school part-time. Three years into living in Paris, I quit my studies and then the job. We had decided to start our family. When I subsequently dropped out of the Parisian stress race, I felt immense relief.

However, it wasn't enough. I couldn't find peace, and I made very few friends. I had imagined soulful and artistic connections and friendships but was surrounded by viciousness and indifference—and lots of misunderstanding. I made an effort to regain my equilibrium by returning to the religion of my childhood. I served in a women's parish organization for a time and was met with more strangeness than I can say. Even the clergy of the parish were wanting; they had no skill in advising and helping people outside of the confines of religious life. I realized then and there that I had set myself up: with my own family and friends far away and long-distance phone calls highly expensive, with in-laws who were distant also, but who lived just across the city, with my young husband who ran the Parisian race for his career. So I began to crack and fall through the many holes of my life. I was going to pieces, and as I did, I continued to fall and did not bounce, for there seemed to be no bottom to this abyss of despair and disappointment. Yet I prodded on, wrestling with these overwhelmingly depressed emotions, still on the same trajectory, trying to make sense of it all. I started to realize that I had cut myself off from my Soul. I was doing NOTHING that I had wanted for myself, nothing that I wished for in my Life. Paris had not been my dream, and I was terribly confused by the direction that my life had taken.

One afternoon, I was alone in the bedroom of our former 10th-floor apartment in the Parisian suburb of *Charenton-Le-Pont*. My baby, R., was in his room for a nap. It was sometime during the fourth year of my being in France. I wasn't feeling as if I were alive. I felt as if I were dying. (No one ever spoke to me about postpartum depression.) I was lost to myself. My soul had flown away, and I no longer knew what it was all about or if I was even real...I had had enough.

I closed the door and threw myself on the floor.

I turned to God, this time. Not to a church, nor to another human being. I had tried and they had failed me. I did pray in Jesus' name, however, being brought up a Christian. I gave it a shot. I tried everything that I could think of to find comfort and release. I sobbed and I cried; I begged for help and talked for an hour amidst tears—to Heaven. I invoked the Holy Spirit; I prayed for Love, Life, Connection, and Creativity. I couldn't cope anymore, and I needed something positive to come into my life to help me. I was so disappointed in everyone and everything. Nothing made sense, and nothing came together. It seemed as if everything was disjunct and out of harmony. I was disappointed in myself, as well, that I hadn't made music my way of life…that I hadn't written the songs of my heart I had longed to write when a teenager, nor was I singing with my most beautiful gift—my lyric voice. I hadn't moved to California, which had been my youthful dream…I was SO FAR OFF THE MARK!

When I was finished, I was emotionally and physically emptied out. I rose up off the floor, blew my nose, wiped my tears, and got on with the day.

Music did make its way back into my life. It started gently, as I sang lullabies to my baby. We had already bought a rocking chair and I sat in it often, especially in the middle of the night, singing to our son as I rocked him. I was overjoyed. Thus I reincorporated music into my daily life and sang my love to our baby. It was a crucial step to becoming whole again.

Then came Spring. By early April 1991, the Earth felt the new stirrings of life, and the Sun was well into Aries, my Lunar sign. We feel the energy speeding up in the Spring, and it was extremely pronounced that year for me. I was working on a project alone in an extra room that we had in our building. I was typing up a newsletter for the church parish women's organization the very week prior to Easter, Holy Week. I was so focused on the project that with these additional ingredients—lack of sleep, lack of proper eating, and too much caffeine, as in, *le café français fort* (strong French coffee). Let me tell you, I'm not a coffee drinker. Tea is my favorite. This French coffee wreaked havoc with my body chemistry.

I went out of my mind.

While seated in a chair, I left this mundane existence. I left my body, too, and connected with another realm. I was seeking help still. It was as much an act of love as it was an act of desperation. It could have been a realm of the Collective Unconscious or a far deeper realm of The Spirit…I don't know. Perhaps both.

Voices. Visions. Poetry fell from my lips. There was one night while I was trying to work on the newsletter when all I did was speak in rhyme in that little room, like some sort of Pythia of The Delphi Oracle. Poetry and prophecy poured out of me. I was experiencing a kind of elation like I was in Heaven. When that week was over, I didn't sleep for seven more nights. That was when I began to deteriorate cognitively. The elation was over. When I went to my usual psycho-therapy appointment, I explained the visions, the various voices and such, along with my exhaustion. My therapist became very upset by it all. I was hallucinating, she explained. Anxiety came on strong and unexpectedly. I was in a tailspin. I went into deep shock, body, and mind. I was in hell.

I remember being so achingly conscious and hyper-aware. It etched itself upon my brain, but it was an overload. Though very aware of all the feelings and experiences, I couldn't always say what was happening. I was burned out.

My therapist said psychosis. I wasn't sure what that meant. So she explained it to me. I was in a state of mania. The voices weren't real; neither were the visions. She said so. It was Manic/Depression.

What now?

My therapist contacted a medical doctor. Medication was prescribed. It took several days for me to come to a state of some mental and physical rest. The medication put me to sleep, finally. Then I couldn't function because I was groggy all the time…always half asleep, and I wasn't supposed to take caffeine in any form. My therapist was still trying to explain to me what had happened, but her explanation didn't quite add up, and I had doubts; something wasn't clear. Also, she insisted that I NOT go to the hospital. She wasn't in favor of me leaving my son. He was 1 1/2 years old. She expressed her thoughts that I should remain home and take care of my son. I was worried, though, by the negative energies that I felt. Was this part of the

Collective Unconscious? However, the therapist's and the doctor's decision was firm. I stayed at home. My cognitive functions were blown, and I couldn't fight their decision. My husband and I listened to their advice. What did we know? So, being unprepared for anything of this sort, we acquiesced.

Yet something was nagging at me: The Voices. They had been different in the beginning. They had been kind and helpful. So much happened. Still, I had gone over the edge. I had so much fear and anxiety. It was hell every day trying to function. I was so sensitive that I couldn't be around people very much and stayed at home. We tried to create a normal routine, B. and I. We had already found a place at the local community daycare center, *la halte garderie,* where I could drop off our son several times during the week so I could attend therapy and doctor visits. This was immensely helpful as we knew no one yet whom we could ask to babysit.

The opposing energies were battling within me night and day. Dark forces sometimes came into my dreams. There were hypercritical, malevolent voices and energies. My fears kept me from sleeping once in a while, despite the strong medication. I thought of the psychological poisons in books that I'd read years before and wondered: why had I needed those ideas or distractions—murder mysteries and fundamentalist reasoning all coalesced into a devil who seemed real, and hell was a place that I was dropped into again and again. Like in the tale of the Mesopotamian Goddess Inanna, I had descended into the Underworld and was proverbially hanging rotten on a hook. I couldn't think…only feel.

Yet, somehow there were glimmers of positive energy, a benign 'Presence.' I felt that there was *something*—maybe God? The Universe? A new friend talked about 'The Universe' as an entity. Perhaps this *something* was actively present and holding me together. I avoided religious activities and bowed out of the parish women's organization. I just stayed home as much as possible and began my path to healing…There were walks with my son in *Le Bois De Vincennes* (The Vincennes Woods) across the street, a huge tract of land that was still intact because French kings had used it as a hunting ground. Today it contains a zoological park, various playgrounds, a charming lake, restaurants, winding paths, and many, many gardens. Its trees and greenery reconnected me with the Earth.

I was puzzled about mental illness. I had questions; never before did I have so many or seek to answer them. So when I could read again, I began with psychology books, trying to understand what the mind is. Then I read about women's psychology and a woman's soul path in development and individuation. This nonfiction road led to spiritual works, then women's spirituality, and more understanding of humanity. Slowly it began to make sense. Then I came across the term 'New Age' in a tract by Christians who thought it was wrong. I couldn't agree. For example, I had already read Astrology books and found it to be a wonderful tool. What was wrong with it? As far as I was concerned, starry constellations glorified the Creator! Such order and cohesiveness displayed in the Universe…

So instead of turning away, I researched and explored *The New Age*. Instead of agreeing with fearful reasoning, I understood that we humans are living in a period of great change, a 'paradigm shift,' albeit a positive one. The word *paradigm* was new to me and I pondered it. Someone or something was instructing me, but they were just outside of my awareness. For example, Astrology helped, as did the theories and writings of Carl G. Jung, but I found that it wasn't just the workings of the mind or psyche, but really the workings of the whole human being that carried me forward in my personal search.

The word that also caught me was—*Energy!* This was a very new concept for me. The term 'New Age' just means a time of great change, really. There were various philosophies, ideas, and practices that were coming together, which are grouped under this term, but these philosophies and ideas are very ancient, and so are the practices. For example, meditation and yoga. How can they be anything but beneficial? They calm a person and help them to live more mindfully, aware of the wonder of Life. Yogis and yogic practitioners do not pack guns. Could it be that all fundamentalists are fear-based and not Love-based? They, the fundamentalists, seem to be obsessed with dogma. Or law. Which is better: dogma/law or Love? To me, law based on fearful energy fails everyone and everything, and law based on loving energy benefits everyone and everything. Believing in the law of sin doesn't show any constructive means to living a better life; it just grinds down the one who is termed 'sinful.' However, the unconditional Love of the Divine is a Law of Creativity and brings a constructive means to living. One learns from mistakes but not to be stoned to death nor cast out…isn't this really what Jeshua (Jesus) had been teaching?

The religion of my upbringing didn't ring true for me anymore: neither in its ideology, in its spiritual expression, or in its practical application. Yet it would be years before I finally broke away from it. I kept going back to it, trying different approaches until I finally understood: for me, it is a thoroughly human institution, thus fallible. It concerns itself mainly with power, and NOT Love. It uses fear to control human beings and doesn't do much to help the faithful to advance spiritually. The theme of *forgiveness*, that is, my forgiving of every hurt and slight that ever happened, would occupy me for years to come. I was on the way to leaving the *victim attitude*, but I would have to go through a lot more before I got to where I could feel safe and out of the darkness into the Light of Unconditional Divine Love.

The 'kind voices' came back into my awareness years later. They revealed themselves to be my *Spirit Guides*. There had been other voices during my breakdown, however, the negative ones subsided with medication.

In 1997 we moved into Paris itself. We unexpectedly found a townhouse with a small garden—a spiritual oasis amidst the desert. I have always treasured connecting with Mother Nature, placing my feet upon Earth's holy ground, and using my hands for tilling and tending. So, I began planting rose bushes in the ground and then in pots. I have grown about 26 of them over the past 26 years, along with a bio-diversity of other vegetation. *Gardening* is one of my saving graces; another is *music,* especially singing. Thus, my inner healing was seeded. It has grown, blossomed, and will come to fruition in a memoir in the next year or so.

Stay tuned for the unfolding…

LAURENROSE EVENINGSONG

LaurenRose EveningSong was born in New Orleans, Louisiana, United States, and grew up in Chalmette (a suburb of New Orleans). She received her B.A. in Fine Arts/Art History from The University of New Orleans in 1983. In 1984-1985 she worked in the French Quarter at a Fine Arts Gallery while living in the Faubourg Marigny neighborhood.

LaurenRose married and moved to France in 1986. First, she did what most ex-patriots do—taught as an English Language Instructor. She also did graduate studies in Art History at La Sorbonne/Université de Paris IV. In 1989, she left work and study to give birth to her son.

In 1991, LaurenRose experienced the first degree of a profound spiritual awakening along with a mental break.

Following this intense spiritual initiation, she studied music privately with Sally Gordon-Mark, then studied vocal technique and song with Amy Lavietes for 11 years. During these years, she was a member of Amy Lavietes' Association—VOICES. This multi-national troupe performed annual private concerts.

LaurenRose continues her spiritual adventures through eclectic personal study, primarily through books and online courses. After working for almost two years at the English Bookshop WHSmith, she trained in Reiki I, II, & III with Valérie Joly. She then certified as an Angel Guide with Kyle Gray in 2020 and as a Therapeutic Singing Practitioner with Eliana Gilad (Voices of Eden) in 2021. She was initiated in 2022 as a Priestess of Sacred Sound with Elsa Field (Priestess of Avalon).

Currently living in Paris, LaurenRose enjoys writing, music, tending roses, and cultivating her "Garden of Awakening."

FREE GIFT

Sound Healing Meditation "Lauren Rose EveningSong for PEACE & LOVE"

10-minute Sound Healing Meditation with Mantra Chant and Peace Song, accompanied by Crystal Alchemy Bowls.

Access the Sound Healing Meditation on facebook at **www.facebook.com/therapeuticsinging**

CHAPTER 10

This Little Light of Mine

By Cindy Fielding-Smith

When I was seven years old, my bestie and I decided it was a good idea to see what would happen if we poked a broom into a beehive.

The hive was in a pampas grass bush right outside the back door of my house. There was a narrow path that led along the back of our house. At one end was the gate my bestie and I would pass through in the trek back and forth to each other's houses.

I have no recollection of how far we got with the broom, as no sooner had we moved the broom even close to the hive than a swarm of bees started pouring out! My bestie ducked straight in the back door to safety, slamming it shut behind her. I chose to run down the path, out the gate, and directly over to her place, all the while being chased by that swarm of bees. My long white hair flying behind me, I ran as fast as I could towards her place. As I approached the curb on her side of the street, I looked back to see that the swarm had stopped chasing me. Puffed and out of breath from fright and running, I ran my hand through my hair, only to be stung by one more bee who was hiding in my hair.

Even now when I look back on that event, I feel inclined to laugh because all I could think about as I ran was how the swarm of bees chasing me looked just like it did in the cartoons I loved watching as a child. I had no concept of how silly and dangerous our plan was, nor how incredibly lucky I had been. One sting, having been chased by a swarm, is remarkable!

Looking back, I believe that day was a gift from the bees—a marker for me to realise that working with beeswax would reactivate the medicine of that sting! To offer me healing from the events of my life which started at that same time. That the bees had placed a specific call for healing, and that they would hold my light for me, that I would inevitably choose to dim until the day Tree House Candles was born.

For the purposes of this story, I am sharing two major turning points, and one life event, that have had a hand in weaving the tapestry of my life. The story above being one turning point, then following below, the life event, and subsequent turning point, becoming a beeswax candle maker. Of course, life is filled with many events and turning points that direct our path…these are some of mine.

Becoming a beeswax candle maker is a dream come true—a dream I never realised was available for me until it happened! I find it so beautiful how our paths weave their way around and through us, always leading us to the medicine we need to heal and grow, back to the light of who we are.

For as long as I can remember, ever since we met 14 years ago, my husband Ian said he wanted to start a candle business called Tree House Candles and make candles. For as long as I can remember, I scoffed at his dream! Dismissed it as unrealistic. With six children between us and both of us working full time, how on earth could it even be possible?

Then a little under two years ago, I met a beekeeper! We talked, and I shared Ian's dream about the candles with him. The beekeeper was most excited and animated, insisting WE give it a go, promptly promising me a slab of beeswax as a gift and asking me to come back in a couple of days to pick it up.

I drove straight home and registered the business Tree House Candles, as Ian had so named it. I then took a picture of the certificate and sent it to Ian at work. He couldn't believe it! He was shocked and delighted that I was even interested, let alone keen, to start this business with him.

In those moments of speaking with the beekeeper and feeling the harmony in his excitement, something instantly awakened in me. I felt an excitement, a knowing, a spark that, through all the years of Ian talking about his dream, had not been alive in me until that discussion took place! It was undoubtedly a perfect synchronistic moment!

And so began Ian's dream…yet as it turns out, it was also mine.

In a million years, I could not have guessed the abundant blessings that we continue to receive since the day Tree House Candles came to life. It was impossible to know what was in store for us in following this dream. I can only say that it is indeed a gift from God!

Since starting to work with beeswax candle making, there has been a profound healing taking place for both Ian and me. A gentle yet overpowering flow of new awareness and life that is slowly dripping into the personal wounds and cracks accumulated throughout our lives.

When I was seven years old, aside from poking a broom into a beehive, my life was turning upside down. My parents were in the throes of a long and loud marriage breakup.

Until my parents began fighting, my childhood was just a regular one. I loved dressing up in Mum's clothes and creating Abba performances with my friends. I loved sitting in what I named the 'little boat' of my dad's bent legs when he lay on the lounge. I loved running around like crazy with my older brother when Mum put her records on. I loved school and playing with my friends in the street. Life was good.

I had always been a very sensitive and aware child. I noticed things about people and their behaviours that I now know others did not see. I knew when they were happy or sad. So, when my parents started to experience the breakdown of their marriage, the world as I knew it naturally began to enhance and deepen my awareness and sensitivity. My radar for their upset was on high alert. My sensitivity to anything they did or said was always on high alert. There is a school of thought that says empaths are born out of trauma. This event was a life trauma that many of us experience in childhood, and it was undoubtedly the start of my life as an empath.

The predominant gift and shadow—that would set my life.

At some point, I decided that seeing and feeling these things about my parents and others meant that it must be my job to do something about them. I decided that being bright when others were in their suffering would not help, but rather would make them feel worse. I had to try to ease their suffering and serve their needs well before mine, always choosing to dim my own light and joy in life to brighten someone else's.

If I could help by speaking kind words and sharing love…by seeing people and being able to help them heal in those moments, why wouldn't I? Growing up an empath has taught me so much about humanity, kindness, thoughtfulness, awareness, human behaviour, and seeing others for who they truly are, with a heart to love and uplift people, regardless.

The shadow side of being an empath is certainly the struggle to offer those same gifts to myself. Offering kindness, thoughtfulness, awareness. Accepting myself for who I am, with a heart of love, and uplifting myself regardless. To show up in the world in the way I want to, rather than as a response to what others are experiencing. To use my voice in the way I want to and do the things I want to do, without having to consider someone else first. This has been, and is, very hard!

After a lifetime of putting myself last, and dimming my light, each time I touch the beeswax and immerse myself in making our beeswax candles, another aspect of ME comes back to life. Another part of shining my own light is revealed. Each day reveals more magic. I truly believe in the medicine of the bees and that, all those years ago, they set the intention to come back around and offer me deep healing when I was ready.

I am discovering a growing desire to take up space in the world now. To give myself permission to love myself unconditionally. The reflection I am offered is the physical world…a mirror of me…as within so without! The way the bees live, as a synarchy with one another, is teaching me the value of my place in the world—not just today, but since the day I was born. Rather than believing I must dim down, I am being shown the magnificent beauty to be found in being here, in the physical, to shine as brightly as I can. I realise nature does not make itself into anything different in this world. It simply is what it is, as it was created. I am that, too.

In an ancient Catholic tradition, it is taught that beeswax candles hold a mystical meaning for all of us. That the beeswax represents the pure body of Jesus. That the wick represents his soul, and the flame, his divinity. I am not Catholic, yet this tradition is what I feel working as a metaphor in my life.

As we work with the beeswax, Ian and I are following what is undoubtedly our purpose in life. By making the candles, we are given the awareness of our bodies, our soul, and our divinity. We are given the courage to offer this to others through our candles. For others to find their way, and without the need to dim ourselves, but rather that, perhaps, our light can enable others to find their own.

This quote from Mahatma Gandhi hangs on our beeswax candle shop front: "A thousand candles can be lighted from the flame of one candle, and the life of that candle will not be shortened."

This is a profound and beautiful quote that we can all take inspiration from. From the deeper lesson offered here, I am learning, and allowing new awareness to drip into the places which have become so familiar that I never realised there was another way. You see, I spent my life, since the age of seven, believing that I had to dim my light to be able to help others. That my light was too much when others were suffering, and so dimming it was the only solution.

Now I realise two things: Firstly, that in some way, shape, or form, my light has always been shining, though I just could not see it…likely I still don't. Secondly, I am learning a new way. I am not required to dim myself or make myself small to accommodate others. I can give myself permission to fully be here!

CINDY FIELDING-SMITH

Cindy happily describes herself as a hearth keeper of the light. Her gentle and patient nature provides warmth and an open door for those seeking their own paths.

She has been 'consciously' devoted to walking the Way of Love for the past 7 years, and continues to hone this skill set as a student and mentor of the Priestess Presence Temple & School of Sacred Arts.

Creating and holding space for others to safely explore and discover their truth continues to be her life's work. With her deep training in the Priestess Presence Temple, Reiki training, Breathwork facilitator training, and working hands on with beeswax, Cindy has activated her 'hands of light' to offer divine healing for her clients, family, and friends.

Crafting pure beeswax candles with her Beloved Husband in their business "Tree House Candles," as well as teaching the benefits of using beeswax candles, has allowed Cindy the expression of a long-awaited dream!

As one who loves the expression of words, both spoken and on paper, Cindy is delighted to be stepping into the arena as an author and thrilled to be opening up to this new chapter (pun intended) of life.

She lives on the Sunshine Coast in Queensland Australia, with her Husband, and 2 dogs, sharing life with their 6 children, all of whom are out adventuring in the world, creating their lives.

Website: www.cindyfieldingsmith.com
Instagram: www.instagram.com/cindyfs1971/
Facebook: www.facebook.com/cindy.fieldingsmith

FREE GIFT

Candle Meditation

Enjoy this ancient, yet beautiful candle meditation. It includes a guide to how to do the meditation, along with a breathing exercise.

Access here: **https://cindyfieldingsmith.com/free-gift**

CHAPTER 11

The Divine Wild Mother: Becoming Sanctuary

By Michele Leeper

It was May of 1997, three years after high school. I stood in a Walgreens, dizzy and wide-eyed, looking at pregnancy tests. Piping out of the overhead speakers was the song "You Can Go Your Own Way" by Fleetwood Mac. I looked around nervously for my rocker guy friend, assuming he was somewhere in the liquor aisle. We had been on our way to see a band play at a local dive bar when I'd requested this detour. I had a strange feeling in my body and a curious knowing that I shouldn't go out drinking that night. I knew on some level that I was pregnant, but I needed proof.

There existed within me a silent longing for a child. I wanted a family of my own as it had been many years and foster homes since I'd had one. I began my self-imposed exile when I left my mother and younger brother in Texas at the tender age of eleven. I got on a Greyhound bus with an old army footlocker and a ten-dollar bill. I rode four days northeast to Wisconsin to meet my dad. Two and a half years later, my dad died of a cocaine overdose, and my mom was sentenced to prison for harboring a registered sex offender. My brother had been given up for adoption. I never saw any of them again.

I lived in five different foster homes before dropping out of high school at eighteen. I was deeply homesick for a home I had never known, and I believed I would have a sense of purpose if I had a child. That night, I discovered I had received my secret wish.

I had a "pretty college boy" boyfriend named Mack, who was attending University of New Mexico for Biology, and we lived in a one-bedroom apartment close to campus. Before we met, I had been in a vehicle accident while on my way to Oregon. At that time, I was living in the alley behind the apartment complex in an old '69 Volkswagen bus, with two cats and two friends. One night, Mack looked me in the eyes, pupil to pupil, and told me that he loved me. Then, he came home from class one day and said he was leaving on a sabbatical. His parents had purchased an open-ended ticket for him to go to Hawaii. I was madly in love with him—and then he was gone. I was devastated and felt abandoned.

A month later, I decided to get on with it and went to New Orleans for Jazz Fest with a group of saucy girlfriends. Mack returned to Albuquerque after a couple of months. He said all he could think about was how much he loved me and wanted another chance. I confessed that I had been with a couple of other people while he had been away and assured him that it was meaningless. We started dating again and chose to live in separate places.

When I was six months pregnant, Mack and I were living together again and attending all my doctor's appointments as expectant parents. I was occupied with reading all the baby books, like *What to Expect When You Are Expecting*. I was contemplating whether to use cloth or disposable diapers, how to make organic baby food, and how to breastfeed. Then one day, I was scheduled to have an amniocentesis done because my baby was not developing normally. The procedure consisted of inserting a long needle—the kind they use for spinal taps—through my belly button to collect amniotic fluid for genetic testing.

I was terrified as I lay in the oversized hospital gown on a hard table covered in white paper. I was freezing and asked if I could cover up with a blanket. I felt like a lab rat, raw and exposed, while random medical students walked in to see the procedure. *Maybe the janitor would also like to pull up a lawn chair and see the show!* I thought. We were shouldering a lot of stressful unknowns, and Mack supported me as best he could. He stood by my bedside and held my hand…a little too tight.

We found out that I had gestational diabetes and that my body wasn't sufficiently supporting the life growing inside me. I felt wrong, inadequate, and confused. I was becoming disassociated from my body and couldn't fully embrace the experience of being pregnant. The doctor informed me that my labor would be induced, and scheduled a premature delivery as this was now a high-risk pregnancy. I was worried but relieved that I would soon meet my baby on the outside of my body.

After sixteen and a half hours of being in this artificial labor—without pain medication—I desperately wanted to be in the water! Every fiber of my being wanted to sit in a warm shower. I felt like a deranged woman, rocking, growling, squatting, and yelling profanities at everyone in the room! I grabbed one of the nurses by her arm and threatened to jump out the window if they would not let me be in the water. I was apologizing, crying, laughing, and cursing repeatedly. My throat felt like I had swallowed a gravel pit and I was given ice chips to suck on.

After eighteen and a half hours, my son was born! I watched the expressions on all the faces of the people around me and started to feel the panic rise within me. Mack was as white as the hospital sheets and was mumbling something to the doctor. I could not hear any cries from my baby as a nurse took him to the other side of the room. Everyone was looking at me nervously, and I remember trying to get off the bed. I was a bloody mess and had cords and IVs attached to me, so I could not get up to see what was happening. Someone was telling me not to worry…that everything was fine. The room was spinning, and the fluorescent lights were burning my eyes. I feared that, at any moment, I was going to pass out, yet my desire to see and touch my baby kept me alert. I felt like I was swimming in molasses. Everything was in slow motion.

One of the nurses finally brought my baby over to me. He was all yellow and filmy, swaddled in a small blanket with pink and blue stripes. His shape resembled a little frog, and I noticed he had six fingers on his tiny left hand. He had four itty-bitty fingers with translucent fingernails and two thumbs shaped like a crab's pinchers. He was three pounds, twelve ounces, and sixteen inches long. His eyes were swollen and covered in jelly. He reminded me of an upset garden gnome, awakened too early in the season, or a tiny mythological creature from the sea. He fascinated me. My mind did not register deformities, only magic and curiosity! The rest of the world disappeared as I held him to my breasts. We already knew each other in spirit, and I knew I would protect him fiercely from this day forward! He was quickly rushed to the Pediatric Intensive Care Unit, where he stayed for a month to be monitored.

I was sent home four days after my son was born, and I felt empty with this new vacancy in my body. We discovered that my baby (whom I had not yet named) was deaf. His cry was as soft as a whisper. He was also diagnosed with Dextrocardia; his heart was flipped in the opposite direction. I spent time at the local library looking up these birth abnormalities and conditions when I wasn't at the hospital nursery, pumping breast milk, or crying inconsolably on the kitchen floor of the apartment. I reflected on the hostility I had come to feel towards those who, in the beginning, had tried to convince me to have an abortion. Mack's dad considered me a criminal for "Fucking with his DNA and family lineage!"

Then, people began to strongly suggest that I give up my child for adoption. The nurses enjoyed gossiping about how I had not even named him yet. His little hospital incubator said, "Baby Boy Leeper." I knew his name would come to me when it was meant to. I first wanted to feel into who he was. I was livid at the notion that I would abandon my son in the way that my mom gave up one of my brothers, who was born with Down Syndrome. All I knew for sure was that this child and I had a karmic contract, and this was our path—whatever that would look like.

I understood, with tremendous clarity, that this spirit chose me as his mother in this lifetime, and I chose him! This, of course, sounded like insanity to the "rational" people around me, who proclaimed that I wasn't fit to carry such a burden at my age…an unmarried mother without parents or family support. Yes, I was young and not quite who everyone else thought I should be, but I didn't bend or break. I had no idea what to expect, and I did not entirely know what I was doing—except that the Divine Wild Mother inside of me did. My son, River Michael Dylan Leeper, was now going to be the biggest adventure of my life!

I did not have a plan. There is almost no way to make oneself ready for this kind of experience, and I felt like I was wandering in the wilderness alone. What I did possess was a particular instinctual courage and soulfulness, despite the repeated attempts to re-make me into someone more acceptable. I regularly encountered rejection, judgment, ignorance, and meanness from others as I learned to navigate being a motherless mother with a special needs child.

At some point, I began to feel like a rabid animal in a corner. Mack had proposed marriage to "do the right thing," but I declined. However, I loved his mom dearly because she was thoughtful and kind, and it was a great comfort to have her around when she would come to visit and help with River.

On the other hand, Mack's dad and older brother treated me like a poor, white-trash gold digger. It was extremely hurtful. I started acting recklessly as I felt increasingly like I was being controlled.

I wanted something more for my life and again was at a crossroads. Albuquerque had become a hungry ghost land for me. Most friends I had made along the way had moved back to wherever they came from or on to somewhere else. I remember walking down the street, drunk on red sangria, crying under the streetlight, and feeling the wind rattling through my ribs. My time there had reached its end. I decided that I was going to move to Portland, Oregon, to begin a new chapter.

Once I had made my declaration, Mack's dad hired a lawyer and demanded a paternity test. Everything after that happened very quickly. I complied resentfully, knowing this could be a prison sentence for me. I went out into the summer night and partied like it was the end of the world.

One morning, Mack said that we needed to talk. His brother and his brother's girlfriend were there. I had spent the night at his place since he was watching River, and I had gotten in late. He handed me a letter. The paternity test had come back negative, stating that Mack was not my son's biological father. I was numb and sick to my stomach. I couldn't say anything and got up from the couch and went back to bed. A couple of hours later, I was playing it all back in my head—like a movie on rewind. It did not make sense to me, because Mack was the only person that I had unprotected sex with. His heartbroken eyes met mine when I finally appeared from my cave. He was feeding my son some oatmeal and a mashed banana when I sat down at the kitchen table.

River was about a year and a half old…a happy little baby with eyes as blue as the Caribbean. The two loved each other very much, and I felt deeply emotionally fragmented and even afraid. I was more terrified by the thought of staying and living a half-life that was not truly my own than answering the call of the unknown. The outside messages I received were that I was crude, unlikely to succeed in life, and wrongheaded. My eyes had lost their moisture and sparkle, and I knew my soul required something different from me. I required more creative nourishment than the places I'd been—internally and externally.

I knew that I would remember this day for the rest of my life. My eyes scanned the room, taking in the warm olive green velveteen sofa, the New Mexico chilies poster, the potted cactuses, Mack's beautiful, tanned skin, and his forlorn Southwest sunset eyes. He was an exceptionally beautiful, intelligent man, but had no backbone. He shivered in his father's shadow. I had lost respect for him along the way. I loved him, yet I was not in love with him.

He pleaded with me to stay, saying that he would marry me and raise River as his own, anyway—as if I required a husband to legitimize the existence of my child! It made me seethe inside, and I felt like my ears were popping from reaching high elevation. Once I returned to my body, I knew that I was free to leave. I packed up my son and drove off into the blazing red sunset, in my sky-blue VW bus. Destination: Portland. The City of Roses!

I felt like I could begin again. Driving with the windows down and the wind in my hair, I felt my instincts returning. No one had to be wrong for me to be right…I only knew that I had to go. I might have arrived in Portland sooner if I had not been in the car accident that turned into a three-year layover in Albuquerque. That had been the plan, but other forces intervened. I clearly was meant to stay and conceive my son. Perhaps in some other multi-dimensional timeline or fantasy, I *did* stay and marry Mack. But I knew in my heart that I had received what I was meant to and could now release what no longer served my highest potential.

My experiences in New Mexico, the Land of Enchantment, were the beginning of a multitude of spiritual lessons. I have cultivated so much compassion for that younger version of myself. Starting a new life in Portland wasn't all cotton candy, rose parades, and sexy sailors. It pushed me past my edges and demanded more from me than I thought I was capable of.

A couple of my soul siblings, who were married, moved to Portland within a few days of our arrival. We had been close when we lived in New Mexico, and they were in the vehicle accident with me that kept us all from moving to Oregon sooner. What I came to realize is that it was all part of the Divine plan. About a year and a half later, after we all moved, these two friends had a son born with Autism. We bonded even more profoundly from having children with different abilities. We supported one another emotionally and shared childcare. The universe supported me further by sending another sister friend from Albuquerque, as well. She lived with River and me so I could go back to school and become a student at the Community College. I utilized Early Intervention Services for my son, and he received care from the best specialists and doctors. He graduated from high school in 2016 with a modified diploma.

It was sometimes overwhelming throughout the years, and I found myself repeating familiar patterns. I became seduced by toxic romantic relationships which tore me down more than they lifted me up. I had a great deal of very ungraceful times that filled me with shame and regret. I had another beautiful son, and I married his dad from a place of scarcity, hoping that I could finally feel a sense of belonging. Along the way, I found the courage to take a stand, learn to love and respect myself, be it, learn it, feel it, unlearn it, and live it—my way. At the heart of it all, I was learning to embody mothering myself, and I became my own sanctuary. My spirit is the temple, and my body the Holy chariot.

I got to shed my skin and grow into my true self. I learned to love myself unconditionally and integrate all parts of me—light and shadow. I started singing, acting, dancing, writing, traveling, and spending more time in nature listening, feeling, and tuning in to my body. I gave up finding ways to numb out and finally made peace with myself. I understood that what I was seeking all along was myself! I became aware that all my experiences happened for me and not to me. Parts of me that were frozen began to melt and surrender to my internal flame of passion.

We are all Divine Wild Mothers. We create! As women, we hold the power to create life. Whether we have children or are re-mothering ourselves, we are the universe seeing itself. My life's purpose is to be a sanctuary and support other wild women to reclaim their freedom, embody personal sovereignty, and remember their Divinity.

MICHELE LEEPER

Michele speaks the language of love. She came into this world as a multi-dimensional old soul, with a raw and colorful sense of humor and a huge compassion for humanity. She is a lighthouse for seekers who desire to cultivate their own inner sanctuary.

Michele's path includes working and volunteering as an Advocate for homeless and runaway teens and supporting other women recovering from addiction and domestic violence.

For over a decade, she facilitated support groups and volunteered as a first responder for women in crisis. As a mother of a differently-abled child, she became a Direct Support Professional within the Intellectual and Developmentally Disabled Community. Michele is an Empowerment Coach **@divinewildmother.llc** and Author. Her current work is a sequel to her debut memoir series, *Daughter*.

Michele lives in the Pacific Northwest with her two sons. On any given day you may find her forest bathing with the trees, mushroom hunting, berry picking, or enjoying the great outdoors at a hot spring or clothing optional beach. She also has a passion for singing, dancing, bodyboarding and traveling with her family and friends. Chasing down the sun by the ocean, is her ultimate happy place!

Learn more at **www.micheleleeper.com**

Let's stay connected!
FREE Discovery call with Michele

Join me for a FREE discovery call to discuss how I can support you in expanding your vision and the possibilities for your life, and to get on the waiting list to receive the first chapter of my memoir series, *Daughter*.

To schedule, email **michele.leeper11@gmail.com**

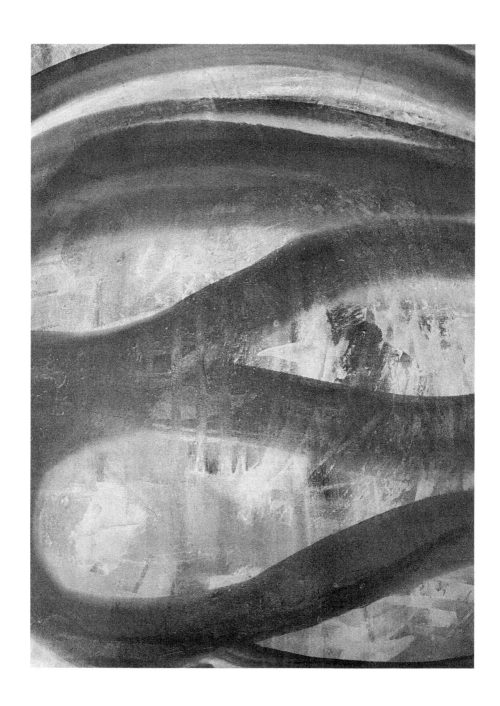

CHAPTER 12

Unmasked: Becoming the Crown'd Crone

By Betz McKeown

MASK. Noun: *1. A covering for all or part of the face, worn to conceal one's identity. 2. Anything that disguises or conceals; a disguise; pretense.* **Verb:** *1. To disguise or conceal; hide; dissemble. 2. To cover or conceal with a mask.*

The day I discovered I was autistic, everything changed. I was 61 years old when the light switch was turned on. So many negative things I had believed about myself dissipated, and other beliefs and feelings I'd experienced now made sense. Many of the jigsaw puzzle pieces of my life and who I thought I was, previously spinning in the air around me, began to land, and the picture of who I *really* am became clear.

Before then, I had no idea I was on the spectrum. The idea had never even occurred to me. Yes, I have always felt different—or, to use the term I learned to embrace and own, *weird*—like I never fit in. But I attributed all that to somehow being broken inside.

The realization that I am neurodivergent happened pretty suddenly. In the span of about two months, four women I knew personally, or whom I followed and admired, disclosed that they were autistic. As I learned from each about their discovery, I was floored. They were all intelligent and well-spoken. They were all compassionate, talented, and dedicated to their work, families, and lives. They were all involved in the holistic health and spiritual communities I belonged to. They seemed to me so regular, so cool, so...*Normal!*

But in relating their respective self-discoveries, their reflections hit home. They, like I, felt *other*—wrong, different, broken. They felt like they never quite fit in. They were always surprised by people's behaviors, responses, and actions. They learned to mimic others' social cues and mannerisms to avoid feeling uncomfortable or standing out. They couldn't relax in their own skin, figuratively and literally.

I was almost always uncomfortable in my physical body. I've been told that even as an infant and a toddler, I didn't like to be held or cuddled, and would scramble out of relatives' hugs. When my mom brushed my hair, it felt like my scalp was on fire and I would scream in pain. (This would explain the terrible pixie haircuts in all my childhood pictures!) I learned to focus my sense of self just outside my body, so if I brought my attention back to me, it was like I was looking at myself from above and to the left. Projecting my inner self outside my body provided an escape from the discomfort of being in a physical form.

For as long as I can remember, I've felt different. People confounded me—I never understood why people would do what they did or say what they said. It seemed like I was always watching them, trying to figure out, anticipate, and copy their actions, emotions, and responses. It seemed I wasn't just from another country but from another planet—watching, observing, and learning what it meant to be *human.*

In trying to fit in, I would become whatever anybody needed me to be. Unfortunately, as is true for so many women on the spectrum, this too often leads to manipulation and abuse. In my case, the sexual abuse started when I was very young. To the best of my reckoning, it began when I was three and continued until I was 12, when I finally realized I could say, "No more!" Somehow, I summoned the courage to stop it despite the fear that the perpetrator would follow through on his threat to hurt my family. And because I didn't want to seem wrong or stupid, I didn't tell anybody about the abuse until I was in my 20s.

Because neurodivergence in women seems more complex than in men, it helps to see the autism spectrum as a pie chart rather than as a linear depiction. It's too easy with the linear representation to make unfair comparisons of how autism individually manifests in different people. The pie-chart model better encapsulates the range and variety of the autistic experience. I completed many online autism assessments, and while they all indicated that I am autistic, the Pie Chart spectrum just makes more sense.

Imagine a pie chart cut into ten slices, each representing a specific autistic trait—Anxiety, Communication Problems, Executive Function, Eye Contact, Meltdowns, Need for Routine, Restricted or Focused Interests, Sensitivities (light, noise, touch, etc.), Socialization, and Stimming. And within those ten slices are scores 1 (low expression) to 10 (high expression). Seeing it represented in this way allows a much more nuanced way to define autism.

Personally, I score very low on Social Issues (I love a good get-together) and Communication Problems (my communication skills are pretty darn masterful, because they've had to be!), but quite high on Physical Sensitivities (loud sounds, hair brushing, and light touch are usually irritating and sometimes painful). I also score high on Executive Function (it's challenging for me to organize routine tasks) and Focused Interests (I cannot learn enough about spirituality, all the different forms of energy healing, and classic rock & roll!). Hearing about stimming (repetitive physical movements or articulated sounds that help to calm and self-regulate the nervous system) first clued me in to the possibility that I might be "on the spectrum." I tap out repetitive rhythms on my fingers, and often accompany the tapping with sounds or notes, usually quietly or silently to myself so as not to draw undue attention.

Neurodivergence, the umbrella term that includes autism and ADHD, is often misdiagnosed or not diagnosed at all in girls and women. Historically, research and testing for autism was exclusively a male diagnosis. Some doctors even now believe it isn't possible for females to be autistic.

There are many reasons why women's autism falls through the cracks of modern medicine. Women more easily learn over time how to hide their symptoms. They are generally better at "masking" (hiding, adapting, or camouflaging), which scientists say women do three to four times more often than men, even within the neurotypical population. But for many autistic women, this masking takes a toll and can result in anxiety or depression. Because of this, women are often misdiagnosed and go on to suffer *autistic burnout*, the long-term psychological and physical exhaustion of simply trying to act normal.

When I was 15, I experienced my first autistic burnout. I was not sleeping. My body was breaking down with constant kidney infections, constipation, and bronchitis. I was suffering from what I now know as clinical depression. I felt exquisitely alone—I had some friends, but while it seemed that I could speak their language, nobody could speak mine, which made me feel unimportant, invisible, and nonexistent. I hit the wall. I got the bottle of Darvon that my doctor had prescribed for my insomnia and swallowed all that was left, about half a bottle. And I laid down and waited to fall asleep in the forever kind of way. And I waited. And...nothing. Not even a little drowsiness. At the time, I was pissed! I was so exhausted, so despairing—I just wanted out. But I'm sure the anger at not even being to die right was the fire I needed to keep me going, at least temporarily. And why didn't the drugs work? I'm convinced now that it was divine intervention. Not the right time, apparently. It seemed I still had way too much to do!

When I was about five years old, my cousin Bob and I were watching a show on our tiny black-and-white TV. Suddenly, Bob was laughing at me, making fun of me—I had been copying the actress's facial expressions and was completely unaware of what I was doing. I now know that I was observing and learning how neurotypical people express emotions, and I was caught doing so. I was deeply embarrassed for doing something so stupid. I felt shame for not understanding what I was doing or why I was doing it, and I began to unconsciously learn how to hide my authentic self. I had started to mask.

Over the years, the masks piled on. In order to fit into the group, the class, the experience, the job, the church, or the club, I would become whatever was expected of me. And I got really good at it. I was the chameleon—I learned how to think like whomever I was with, behave like them, talk like them, and believe like them. I could relate to everybody's point of view without ever realizing I didn't have an opinion of my own.

What are masks, exactly? Masks are generally the roles one takes on, either consciously or unconsciously. They can also be behaviors, identities, traits, jobs, etc. Masks can be imposed upon you by your family, community, society, church or religion, school or education, or employment. You may also choose them for yourself. Or some combination of the above. For example, your culture may expect you to be the Mother, as may your family, and it may be a role you also choose for yourself.

Some masks are adaptations resulting from trauma. For example, a common adaptation is the abused child who grows up to be the Perpetrator. This type of trauma-based adaptive mask is often used to create safety in its limiting yet singularly efficient way. Or conversely, the child may remain the Victim, which is simply an unconscious habit they haven't found a way to break.

Many masks appear as dual roles: Perpetrator/Victim, Madonna/Whore, Good Girl/Bad Girl. Some masks are judged as elevated: Mother, Wife/Spouse/Partner, Expert. Some are considered negative: Loser, Tramp, Black Sheep, and Rebel. Some are viewed with pity: Outcast, Wallflower, or the Persecuted One. Some are seen as enviable: the Sexy One, Golden Child, or Popular Girl. However they are viewed or worn, these masks are camouflage for both neurodivergent and neurotypical women to hide their sacred, authentic, seemingly vulnerable selves behind.

The most insidious mask I unconsciously coveted was "Normal," that ever-moving target and slippery ideal that changes with the circumstances, the people, the job, etc. What made it even worse was that it was always and only what *I thought* was normal. But in my unaware mind, Normal felt like the safest place to be. I could hide the truth of myself inside Normal. I could be accepted and have real friends as Normal. I wouldn't draw unnecessary and unwanted attention as Normal. The desire to be Normal was an unattainable goal that kept me locked in a loop of persistent inauthenticity for the better part of my life.

Long before my *Autism Realization Breakthrough* (as I fondly call my discovery), I could feel there was more to me than the Broken Victim I thought I was. I had done decades of self-development, personal growth, and healing. I had explored my traumas and integrated my shadow. I had used my own healing, training, and experience to create ever more effective techniques and programs for my clients.

But it was in discovering my autism that the real transformation began. And it was immediate! I felt instant relief. Suddenly, my entire life made sense. There was a tremendous sense of freedom in finally realizing that I was NOT broken but that my brain simply processes information differently. I was nervous about how others might react to my new-found revelation. A few people did not deal with it gracefully and made themselves scarce. Despite that, I'm still the same person, and my overwhelming internal reaction was—and is—gratitude and happy acceptance.

As I began to release the roles and masks that didn't feel aligned with my True Self, a sense of divine discontent rose in me. I just couldn't be inauthentic anymore. Despite the positive intention of masks to keep us safe from what we view as threats, there was a rawness of those lifelong little *t* and big *T* traumas, which could finally be more easily integrated once exposed to the light of awareness and understanding.

It was obvious that I was to include *unmasking* in my toolbox of healing techniques: identifying what masks I wear, when I wear them, how they make me feel when I put them on, and when I remove them. What roles did I play, in what circumstances, and with whom? The unmasking turned out to be the most intense self-discovery journey that I'd ever set out on. And that's saying something, as I've spent my entire life pursuing *Who I Really Am*. And now I get to use that same unmasking tool with my clients so that they, too, can reclaim their authentic, empowered, sovereign, sacred feminine selves.

The fact that all this unmasking started during my crone years is, I'm sure, no accident. There's something about this phase of life (peri-menopausal/menopausal/post-menopausal) when we're more willing to confront our self-identities. "Who the hell am I? What am I doing? What do I want to do? Who do I want to be?" The answers to these questions are hiding under the masks we've worn our entire lives.

The ElderWise Woman, the Sovereign Queen, the Crown'd Crone—these identities are our birthright as we age into our innate wisdom. As women—neurodivergent and neurotypical—we have earned the right through our lived experience to don that mantle. To claim it, though, means taking a hard, honest look at how we've not owned our authentic identities. That means knowing your masks. (This inquiry can begin at any age, although being at the Crone phase myself, I have found it to be an especially rich and revealing journey.)

You might begin by looking at the masks you wanted to wear or thought you wanted to wear: Did you always want to be the Mother? The Wife? The Partner? Then explore how those roles lived—or didn't live—up to your expectations. Did you keep those masks on? Did you remove them? Were they removed by someone else? How did all that feel?

What other masks have you worn? What masks were expected of you by others? Which masks did you expect of yourself? Did you ever question them? How did you feel about them at the time? Looking back, how do you feel about them now?

Would you decide now, with your new wisdom, to choose to take on any of those roles again? If yes, which ones still appeal to you? Why would you want to wear that mask again? How might you wear it differently? And, if there's no desire to revisit a previous role, why not? How did it not serve you?

There are no right or wrong answers, only curiosity, exploration, and awareness! There is so much opportunity for inquiry when you begin to explore your masks. Once you identify and remove them, you will start to see your authentic self and create the change in your life that reflects the truth of your sovereign self.

While you are not the masks you wear, you may want to put some of those masks back on occasionally. I do that sometimes! Depending on the circumstances, I may decide to put on the mask of the Host, Mentor, or Best Friend. And I will always joyfully wear that *Granzi* mask (that's what my grandkids call me)! Knowing that you can choose when, where, why, and with whom to mask up is so empowering. At this phase of knowing who we are—and who we aren't—our conscious masks can be an extension of our authentic sacred selves, instead of representing the unawareness of how we show up in and navigate the world.

BETZ MCKEOWN

Betz McKeown has played many roles and worn many masks: Daughter, granddaughter, niece. Wife, mother, grandmother. Friend, antagonist, competitor. Student, initiate, apprentice. Victim, survivor, thriver. Healer, coach, counselor. Teacher, mentor, author. Priestess, witch, alchemist. Maiden, Mother, Crone.

Who she really is, though—under the masks and aside from the roles—is an embodied soul who has lived a full, painful, rich, difficult, joyful, terrifying, redemptive, integrated life. In the process, she has healed personal trauma, removed myriad masks, and reclaimed her Authentic Sovereign Self. And she is deeply committed to guiding other womxn in doing the same.

Betz has been an integrative health care provider for over 30 years, offering energy and vibrational medicine, health and transformational coaching, spiritual counseling, intuitive guidance, and sacred oil anointings, as well as classes, workshops, and programs that strengthen her clients' optimal health, inspire their personal and soul evolution, and awaken their inherent Sacred Feminine Sovereignty. In addition to her private practice, she was employed as an Energy Medicine Provider at Wake Forest Baptist Health's Integrative Medicine Center in Winston-Salem, NC working primarily with veterans through the Veterans Administration. Her trainings and certifications include Reiki, Healing Touch, Esoteric Healing, EFT/Tapping, Somato-Respiratory Integration, Integrative Nutritional Health Coaching, Transformational Coaching Method, and Rosa Mystica Scent Priestess training.

In her current phase in life as the ElderWise Womxn, Betz is redefining her practice as a virtual and physical sacred sanctuary through the YshaYe Sacred Rose Temple to provide healing, integration, education, and sisterhood for all womxn, employing the healing arts of Somato-Energy Integration, Feminine Sovereignty Guidance, Holy Oil Anointings and personalized Alchemical Blends, Oracular EmpowHERment Readings, and The Crown'd Crone Circle membership.

"Join me, Sister—let's reawaken our authentic and empowered sovereign selves, restore the energy of the Sacred Feminine within, and in doing so, bring balance and purpose back to our personal lives and the world at large."

To connect with Betz and to see what she's up to these days:
www.betzmckeown.com/
www.facebook.com/YshaYeSacredRoseTemple/

FREE GIFT

Unmask Your Authentic Self: An Exercise for Sacred Feminine Empowerment & Sovereignty

A simple and deeply effective technique to begin to identify and release your masks of inauthenticity and step into the sovereign queen you were born to be!

Access here: **https://attractwell.com/BetzMcKeown/ landing/unmask-your-authentic-self**

CHAPTER 13

My Cosmic Antenna: How Hair Trauma Led to Loving Myself

By Laura Sullivan

Think back. Have you ever experienced a hair disaster at some time in your life?

It may have happened with a hairdresser, your mother, a friend, or even with your own hands. Often occurring just before school photo day, many of us have dealt with hair that's been cut too short, a horrific style, or even a color or perm process gone awry. Who could imagine this most unwanted, even traumatic, event would lead me to discover one of my greatest joys and life purpose? No, I did not become a hairdresser.

It happened in the early days of my acting career in Los Angeles. For the previous five years, I'd lived in New York, working for ABC Television and several independent producers. I thought my work would remain forever behind the scenes. But then, the writers of one television series said I must move to Los Angeles if I wanted to work for them. So, I did. Once there, opportunities unfolded that led to acting work, and I discovered— surprise, surprise—that I loved it. So, my focus shifted to acting classes and auditioning for film, television, and stage.

In addition to the entertainment industry, Southern California was a mecca for holistic healing, bodywork, and enlightened sexuality; areas of self-exploration I enthusiastically embraced, practiced, and wanted to study further. One event I attended was a weekend seminar in the living room of John Gray, who went on to write *Men Are from Mars, Women Are from Venus.* He and his partner were teaching ways to have more conscious relationships. Another participant, William Mercury Yount, shared his holistic practice of working with hair based on sacred geometry. He called it "Hair Balancing." I found it most intriguing and wanted to know more.

My long, straight hair had lots of body and shine when I lived on the East Coast, but it was not responding well to the air and water of Southern California, where it became a daily challenge.

I had recently been cast as the lead in the play *A Thousand Clowns,* and the four-month run was scheduled to open in eleven days. Although I needed help, I couldn't risk my hair with some New Age, "woo-woo" hair experience. Who knew what might happen?

I hoped a light body wave could help manage my hair for the four months of the play. So, I went to the Beverly Hills hairdresser who had given me a successful trim a few months before. He assured me he knew what he was doing and that I should sit down and be quiet. Unfortunately, he left the perm solution on my head way too long, and burnt my hair to a crisp! It was unsalvageable.

Then, the disaster was made worse by having to chop it all off. I was left with three inches of frizzy, Brillo-Pad hair. It was hideous. That's when I called "Mercury" asking if he could please do the "Hair Balancing" process he had talked about. I told him I had very little hair left, but he assured me he could "balance it to the longest length"—whatever that meant.

This Hair Balancing was unlike any haircut I had ever experienced. I'd always thought that hair was just dead cells hanging off my head. Everyone believed that. But if that was true, how could I be feeling the trauma from the perm and hideous haircut actually being lifted out of my hair? As he performed the sacred geometry pattern, section by section, I felt sensations of relief and release. It was truly incredible. Never before had I felt life force moving into my head and literally out through my hair. Who knew my scalp and hair were this aware?

Even more amazing, after a few Hair Balancings when the damage was completely gone, my previously straight hair grew in with natural curls and waves! It has remained so ever since. Impressed with the results of this technique, I wanted to continue it forever. Unfortunately, at that time in the United States, the hair industry was obsessed with perms and other chemical processes. So, Mercury spent most of the next decade working in Europe, where they appreciated the excellence of his precision system. He was acclaimed and written about in several countries. I asked him if he would teach me enough of his system so that I could manage my own hair while he was away for such long stretches of time.

He said he would not be teaching until he became famous. But in a rare moment when he needed some fast cash, he offered me the opportunity, and I jumped at it. This was for the pure self-preservation of my own hair; I had no plans of doing this healing art professionally.

Learning the Sacred Geometry pattern came easily to me. It felt like I had done it in a past life. And I felt such joy in performing it—almost like a moving meditation—that I couldn't help sharing it with some close friends and family.

Mercury and I worked with each other whenever he was in town, always increasing my skills. I began to understand that balancing hair is similar to carving a piece of wood. It's about carefully removing what is not needed to reveal the inherent beauty. As a healing art—it opens the flow of energy from the meridians in the body up into the scalp and out through the hair. I witnessed the positive effects on all kinds of hair and on the energetic fields of many people, with Kirlian photography measuring their fields both before and after. I discovered that a haircut can create trauma, or it can create a sense of integration and well-being.

Then in 1990, a time so dangerous that our State Department warned against visiting Peru, Mercury went on a vision quest to Machu Picchu. The man driving him to the ruins was the last person known to see him alive. His murder remains a mysterious and tragic loss. Some of his clients in Southern California who knew that Mercury had trained me in his Healing Art of Balancing Hair sought me out, seemingly desperate to continue receiving this remarkable service. With Mercury gone, how could I refuse?

The '90s was not a strong decade for women in film. It was dominated by action-adventure films catering to males in developing countries, with very few roles for female characters. I gradually spent less energy in the entertainment world and spent more time in the holistic healing world performing Hair Balancing sessions. I made a commitment to keep it alive and pass on this sacred healing knowledge. I began training people both in the United States and Europe. The more I practiced this work, the more information was given to me about the true nature of hair.

I want you to know that your hair is not a collection of dead cells hanging off your head—hair is a vital part of your whole being. Healthy hair is alive and conducts life force. The DNA of our hair is a unique identifier. Each hair on our body and head is actually part of our nervous system, constantly transmitting information to our brains.

Yes, take that in.

Every hair has its own oil gland and its own erector pili muscle. Have you ever felt your hairs standing on end? These tiny muscles are what make that happen. It's a way of signaling...often excitement or danger. Our hairs are capable of picking up and transmitting information to us and about us before we are close enough to make eye contact. Of course, our hair creates a strong visual impression, but it is active at many subtle levels, as well. The tiny hairs vibrating in our ears are what allow us to hear. Our hair connects us with all of humanity.

I noticed that when I wasn't feeling well, my hair was rather drab and lifeless. Sure, I could coax it into shape using styling products, but I could see it was actually a barometer of my internal health. I saw how hair responded differently to various diets, preferring less sugar and more protein, fruit, and vegetables.

I also saw and felt the changes from exposure to different quality waters. Some wealthy clients with fabulous estates in Malibu had well water. It was so hard with minerals it seriously damaged their hair. These people had to wash their hair at health clubs in town or buy bottled water for home hair washing. The same thing happened to friends moving to different parts of the Southwest. Hard water can be extremely tough on your hair, skin, and your health in general.

The upside of the awful water in Southern California was that it spurred my interest in water purification systems and I eventually discovered methods that actually restore the life force back into water. The water we drink internally and the water we wash with have a dramatic influence on the health of our hair and body. In most places, extra filtration is essential to avoid the damage of chlorine and hard minerals, but much more can be done to create truly healthy water.

One of my most dramatic lessons about hair came as a result of two-thirds of my hair falling out. Life was flowing along swimmingly. I had recently finished a feature film starring Rob Lowe, and then I became pregnant with my first child—a most happy development.

The pregnancy was blissful. The water birth that we planned assisted by an expert midwife who had experience with over 300 water births. Everything was in place for a joyous event. Then eleven hours into labor, before I was dilated enough to get into the tub, the midwife suggested we all rest for a few hours to renew our strength. A few hours later, when she came to check on me, the baby had no heartbeat.

We rushed to the nearby hospital, hoping there was some mistake but, tragically, he was gone.

It is beyond challenging to push out a beloved child you know is dead, and yet it had to be done.

Both the midwives and the obstetrician believed they had removed the afterbirth completely. Unfortunately, small bits of it remained, causing me to hemorrhage for the next three weeks. The doctor assured me a simple D&C would resolve the problem, and that the procedure should take ten minutes and I would be home in two hours. That was until he punctured my womb with his instrument. Now I was hemorrhaging everywhere. They brought me to consciousness only to get my permission to put me back out and save my life. It required more doctors and two more surgeries. I was in the hospital for eight days.

As you can well imagine, the stress I experienced was physical, psychological, and emotional. I was a wreck. I felt 90 years old, only able to shuffle half an inch at a time, but I was determined to recover. Week by week I was still sad, but stronger.

Then my hair fell out.

Yes, I knew that hair could fall out due to stress, but this lived experience was worse than anything I imagined. Every morning there were piles of hair on my pillow that I had to pick up and throw away. Meanwhile, my once luxurious hair now appeared like a thin veil. I kept cutting it shorter and shorter so it wouldn't be so obvious, but it looked pathetic. I cried to God at the unfairness, "You have taken my baby and now you take my hair!" How could I tell anyone about this wonderful, life-enhancing hair care system when, suddenly, I had no hair?

I learned that all types of stress burn through B vitamins and minerals like wildfire. These happen to be important building blocks for hair. When a body is experiencing any kind of stress—physical, mental, emotional, or psychological—it withdraws energy from the hair as an act of survival. In its wisdom, our bodies decide that we can live without hair until our stress subsides, when we can renew an abundance of nutrients to send to the hair once again. So, I began ramping up my B vitamins, certain minerals and herbs, and made myself eat healthy food even though I had little appetite. Eventually, I saw new little hairs emerge. The relief at their return was tempered with the knowledge that they would only grow half an inch per month, the normal growth rate, so I would need patience as my crowning glory restored itself.

The upside of this disaster was learning that hair loss is a very common occurrence after a high-stress situation, usually reaching its peak about two months following the event. So, with the next two traumatic ordeals in my life, I anticipated my hair would fall out again. I was able to intercept my body's plan to withdraw nutrients from my hair, by flooding my system with more of those nutrients I knew it needed. I did lose some hair each time, particularly after another surgical nightmare. Fortunately, neither time was as extreme as the first because I employed all the esoteric techniques I had learned the first time, sooner—saving much of my hair.

My experience taught me that hair actually has a consciousness. It responds to the products and practices we use, and to the thoughts and words we use to describe it. Most people describe their hair by the qualities they least like. For example, my hair is too straight, too curly, too thin, too thick, it's falling out, or turning gray. We tend to reaffirm these qualities, defining our hair with these negative terms. Our beliefs and thoughts are powerful foundations of our reality. If we insist on describing our hair by our frustrations and disappointments, it has little chance to become the hair we love. Your hair truly wants to please you, and wonderful transformations are possible. But, if your hair always hears how "bad" it is, it has little hope of changing.

Each day as I cleared the fallen hair from my bed, it was impossible not to think, "My hair is falling out." That was not the reality I wanted to continue living, so I forced myself to focus on the hairs that were still on my head, thanking them for being there and asking them to please stay and multiply. I cut out a picture from a catalog of a woman with hair as long and thick as mine used to be. I taped it to my bathroom mirror, and each time I washed my face or brushed my teeth, I pointed to the picture and told my hair that this is where we were heading. It truly helps to create faster results when your hair and your brain understand and can see what you want.

You may not believe this, but when my hair got as long and as thick as the picture, it stopped growing. I thought, "Oh no, what now?" My husband asked if I had checked in with my hair, which hadn't occurred to me until he suggested it. I questioned my hair and it answered, "Isn't this what you wanted?" I realized the photo, which was once a motivation, was now serving as a limitation. I took down the photo and my hair resumed growing again. The great news about stress-induced hair loss is that when your stress is lessened and your nutrients are increased, your hair can grow back! I know this deeply because I lived through it three times.

Even if you are not pleased with your hair, it is important to find at least one quality that you can appreciate about it. For some people, it is merely that they have hair, after realizing that no hair could be worse. And, although it may sound silly, it's important to tell your hair what you like about it. Praising your hair when it is doing what you like is an important way to teach your hair to become the hair you love. And since your brain is not always distinguishing between what is real and what is imagined, I am a fan of acting "as if." Tell your hair, "I love how fast you are growing," or "I love these new waves." Whatever you desire, give thanks for it happening now. Your thoughts and your words will influence how your hair evolves.

Remember, your hair is with you throughout most of your life…day and night. Do you love it? Or do you battle with it, trying to force it into submission? Do you subject it to toxic products and harmful practices? Would you do these things to your skin…another precious, vital part of your body? Probably not.

Try treating your hair with the tender, loving care you would give a new puppy or kitten. Would you carelessly snip off their whiskers?

Learning to love your hair can be a spiritual practice, an important step in self-care and self-love. How can we truly love ourselves if we hate our hair?

I believe hair is our cosmic antenna. The healthiest hair is usually the most beautiful, exuding radiance and life force. The healthier it is, the better it can perform its esoteric functions in addition to looking and feeling great. Experiencing not just how your hair looks, but how it feels, is one of the amazing gifts of Hair Balancing, as well as enjoying a holistic relationship with your hair. When you become loving toward the hair you have, you allow it to become the hair you love.

LAURA SULLIVAN

Laura Sullivan, the creator of "Hair Harmonics," is a world-recognized expert in holistic hair care. She has practiced and taught the ancient healing art of Hair Balancing, based on the principles of sacred geometry for over 35 years.

In her book, *Awakening Hair, Caring for Your Cosmic Antenna* she illuminates little known truths about hair that the conventional hair industry doesn't want you to know. This new information can be life-changing. Last summer she recorded the audio version of the book for a delightful listening experience.

In her Hair Harmonics training programs, Laura facilitates other "lovers of hair" to learn how to work with hair in ways that uplift the well being of the clients, their hair, the practitioners, and the environment.

Currently, the hair care industry can be quite toxic to hairdressers, their customers, and the environment. Yet, a healthier, more life-enhancing approach exists. When people find it, they never want to go back. You are finding this path now and can introduce others—uplifting the self-esteem, health, and beauty of this world one person at a time.

Laura is available for Consultations, Classes, Talks, and Private Sessions. For more information contact Laura through **HairHarmonics.com**

A HALO for You: New Ways to Understand and Appreciate Your Hair

Laura shares little known realities about your hair that will change how you think about it, work with it, and feel about it.

Humans are not symmetrical. For many of us, this manifests quite dramatically in our hair. Is one side easier to manage than the other? Does one side appear fuller? Do you have cowlicks that defy attempts to tame them? These are normal conditions that can be appreciated as features when you understand them and learn how to work with them. 'A Halo for You' will do just that, offering easy tips and insights that will bring more harmony to your hair.

Access here: www.hairharmonics.com/turning-point

CHAPTER 14

I'm Just Fine

By Star Thomas-Wyse

"'No, I'm fine. And yes, I mean that sort of FINE,' said Reine-Marie, making reference to the title of one of Ruth's poetry books, where FINE stood for Fucked-up, Insecure, Neurotic, and Egotistical."

—Louise Penney, *The Nature of the Beast*

I started caregiving for my folks, Mom with Alzheimer's and Dad with Parkinson's, in 2006. It was a decision I made with tremendous education and information. I had read what books there were at that time and talked to the Alzheimer's Association. I had about 30 years of healing and energy work under my belt and was praised as a natural caregiver with the intuition and insight to fill in the blanks. How hard could it be, really?

Oh, dear reader, if you have never embarked on this kind of journey, I can tell you that my level of naiveté at the beginning of this Mount Everest climb was laughable. I was optimistic and determined that the end-of-life journey with my parents would be full of joy, love, and gentle aging. Somehow, we would go skipping off into the sunset of their life doing all the things we loved, holding hands, and possibly stopping to picnic along the way.

My positive personality was in complete denial of the road ahead. And, if truth be told, I start all my great life adventures in this way—full of optimism! I just default to the belief that my smarts will carry me through, which is often true. But there are times, like this one, when I am abruptly reminded that I truly have no idea what I'm really facing, and my powerful brain, full of information, is just not going to get me the results I'm seeking. You see, underneath all that optimism, I am a giant control freak!

The beginning of this journey started with a trip to visit my folks in sunny southern California and drive their unused car back to Kansas City, where I lived. I was traveling there with a friend of mine for Labor Day weekend, and then we would take a couple of days to drive halfway across the country back home. I was excited to show my friend the ocean—she had never been—and to hug my folks. In the two days we visited with them, I saw and discovered things that left me in total disbelief, jerking me violently out of my denial.

I knew there had been a diagnosis of Parkinson's for my father and, recently, Alzheimer's for my mother, but the experience of chatting with them over Skype was utterly unlike the face-to-face experience. Dad's tremors were worse than I knew, and I discovered he had stenosis of the spine, which meant he listed to one side and could no longer stand straight. Although that was concerning, his full, intact mental faculty was a deep comfort, even though he was in total denial about how much Mom was struggling. I don't blame him, but covering for her was exhausting him and made it difficult for me to initially understand the full extent of what we were dealing with.

Milk put in the pantry by the cereal, soup left on the gas stove top to boil away, the repetition of conversations within a few hours, and not remembering how many verses of the church hymn she had already played were some of the things that I witnessed in those 2 1/2 days.

I spent the entire drive from Los Angeles to Kansas City confirming with my friend that I had not made up what I saw and experienced. Shock makes it nearly impossible to comprehend reality, and I kept rationalizing so I could run away. My friend gently kept bringing me back to reality. Honestly, even though my words were in sync with her calm, steady acknowledgment and truth-speaking, I was spinning out of control and would continue to spin for more years than I could imagine. My way of dealing with that kind of emotional upheaval is to craft a plan so I can be in control. That always works well, right?!?

Sometime in 2008

It was the second time I had put myself in a time-out that day. My ability to handle the constant repetition from my mom had reached the very end of my very last nerve. I had started the practice of putting myself in time-out to avoid losing my entire mind, but the truth is that even time-outs weren't working anymore. My last nerve was constantly frayed, and reaching the end of it required nothing more than anyone breathing in my general direction.

I was a hotbed of a mess. Stressed beyond all recognition and short-tempered, I could erupt volcanically or disintegrate into a blubbering puddle at any time. And I mostly erupted volcanically. I'm not really one to cry. I use profanity liberally, scream at the top of my lungs, and usually take all my frustration out on whoever is handy. To avoid devastating every single relationship I had, I began to erupt on the 11 billion phone calls I had to make to resolve every damn issue of managing their life. I took out a ton of emotional stress on unsuspecting and undeserving phone workers whose job requirements interfered with managing aging parents.

Seriously, I was completely unprepared for how much I would have to deal with and how utterly exhausting it would be trying to get Dad to help me while managing Mom's confusion. Dad would not ever lie to her, and when I tried to bypass Mom to accomplish anything, Dad would block me. We would spend hours in futile conversation until the end of the business day, and I was left with nothing accomplished, everyone tense, and needing to do it all over again the next day.

This was my life—my parents and their incredibly complicated care.

Make no mistake; there were amazing blessings and wonderful moments of true joy during this time. But the overwhelming sense of responsibility that rested squarely on my shoulders grew heavier day by day and, some days, hour by hour.

Have you heard the story of the toad in the pot of simmering water? He is in a pot with a fire under it, and the water is comfortably warm, and he thinks to himself, "This is just fine," and as the temperature increases slowly, he continues to think, "I'm just fine," and then suddenly he's dead.

Yeah, I was certainly that toad, telling myself, "This is just fine; I'll be okay." No matter how many people told me I was suffering from caregiver burnout, I kept telling myself they did not understand. I had excellent help, so I would be fine even if this moment was incredibly difficult.

My basic life pattern is this: Sacrifice everything for the greater needs of those around me. That was my deeply ingrained upbringing. You loved your neighbors first. Or, in this case, my parents.

I had given up nearly everything...my business, friends, spiritual community, and leadership roles. I had even moved into a townhome with my parents, which did not have a tub, giving up my preferred way to reset at the end of a long day—and my days were longer than I could imagine. No matter what I created to support myself, even taking weekends away every couple of months for self-care, the empty core of me could not be filled. My time away felt like putting a thimble of water in a dry well. That tiny patch of dirt felt refreshed, but no water was available anymore, and I could not nourish my parents or myself. But I'm fine; I'll be okay.

November 2, 2009

Mom died in a full-care facility. In the moments of grief, while making a call to the company that Dad and Mom had paid for to handle all the arrangements at the time of their deaths, I discovered that what Dad understood was not the case. They would not come to the facility and pick up the body and take care of everything. That was not the plan he had purchased. So I left my sister and my dad to grieve in Mom's room and went to the nurse's station to discuss and, hopefully, get a resolution. And once again, the volcano erupted, albeit quietly, so as not to disturb the staff. Even at that moment, when all I wanted was to say goodbye, I was in caregiver hell. No opportunity to just *be* because the burden of caring is crushing, and sometimes the end of life is cruel to the living.

December 11, 2009

Five and a half weeks later, Dad died at home after a few days in the hospital with pneumonia.

I felt like an orphan. No support system to count on, no one to save me in a crisis, and no one to bail me out of anything stupid I might do. (I had done a billion stupid things up to that point!)

Approximately three weeks later, right after New Year's, my back went out, and I could not walk without assistance for several days. My pain level was astronomical. I needed to be cared for, and that was horrifying to me. What if I never regained my abilities and capability to care for myself? I could not imagine being dependent.

Fortunately, that did not happen. It was a long four months, but by April, I could work, and life had promise again. Well, let me rephrase that…I was once again in complete denial and living my life as if everything were fine.

August 2013

I was packed and embarking on what was to be a year of world travel since the folks had both passed—a great thing to do for my 60th birthday. Wow, 60! I had researched everything, as usual…read books, watched movies and numerous YouTube videos, read tons of blogs, and was as prepared as anyone could be to embark on this kind of adventure. (Recognize a theme here?) So armed with all my information, I created my itinerary. First, I would travel for a month to visit friends and family on my way to broader horizons and faraway countries.

I have traveled a fair amount in my life. When I was a child, my family lived in Norway. My folks lived in England for several years after I graduated, and my sister moved to Germany right after graduating college. I visited them numerous times and traveled across the United States to see friends and family on several occasions.

I felt confident leaving on my adventure until I got on the Greyhound bus. My first ever trip on a bus, and I had no idea how to navigate the bus terminal! So I was not expecting to be dropped off and feel my heart pound, and my hands get sweaty after my ride left.

That would not be the first time I would question my sanity. All my United States travel was in my car unless flying to a distant location. I feel a sense of safety in my car, a feeling of control. I have my own music, no one else to make space for or listen to, just me and the road. The bus, however, was full of sounds, smells, and people, and I immediately felt SO CROWDED. Little did I know that this was just a precursor to what was to come.

India was more overwhelming than I ever could have imagined. When I finally got through customs and headed toward the airport exit, I nearly turned around and bought a ticket for the first flight anywhere. The noise, the smell, and the chaos were assaulting. If I had not seen my friend frantically waving at me from across the parking area, I would never have stepped foot out of the airport. All the plans I had made, all the research I had done, all the blogs I read, and no one had ever said that you might feel a sense of panic and that, if you are a control freak, traveling alone to a third world country for the very first time might not be the best option. I am sure my heart did not stop pounding for the entire two months I was in India.

The spiritual deepening process I was in for the last month was full of opportunities to lean into greater trust. I failed every time, unable to close my eyes and trust the Divine, unable to still the panic that I was not worthy somehow—every moment crafted for opening to spirit and awakening the feelings of the heart left me in a mild panic and feeling of hollowness—more dread than love. To say that I struggled internally is an understatement.

I thought I was taking this trip to celebrate a birthday milestone, to celebrate making it through some of the most challenging years of my life, and yet there was zero celebration in my heart. I had moments of joy with the other attendees, but hearing their stories of release, trust, and awakening just made my emptiness increase in its vastness until it nearly consumed me. Oh, I fought it—I flat-out lied and told all the stories of healing and growing and increased trust, but none of that was happening. And I would not admit it to anyone, especially myself. I must be okay, remember? Still being the toad in the simmering pot!

Going to New Zealand and meeting up with my sister was a relief. She took over travel plans, and I wasn't alone, so as I started to feel safer, I got more control-y (That's a new word I just made up!) Of course, as is usual with my controlling nature, I got bitchy and we ended up having a knock-down, drag-out fight about the stupidest thing, nearly breaking us apart as sisters. (We've done this often throughout our lives, but this time, we were orphans, only had each other, and were stuck together in one car in a foreign country.) I'm 59.5 years old at this point, and I am still throwing temper tantrums because I can't get my way! Then something in me broke. While losing my mind and volcanically erupting all over my baby sister, I broke inside. Even though we mended the rift between us and went on to finish the last part of our trip, something inside was irrevocably broken.

At the end of our journey, as I was deciding where I wanted to travel next, my back issue from four years prior popped up, not bad enough to derail me but bad enough to force me to stop and cut my travel short and head home. I finally learned I was not okay and needed to get out of the simmering pot before I died or was permanently disabled.

Slowly, over the last ten years, I have recovered from the depth of nearly all-consuming grief, and everything else that was buried has come to light. I have learned to stop saying, "It's fine," and have embraced genuine self-care. As I have returned to my life's passion for healing work and coaching, every client has taught me more about self-care. As I have found greater ways to meet the needs of my clients, I have learned to apply those techniques to myself and my life. I now live from genuine self-care, not self-repair. You see, I had learned to live at the utter expense of myself, giving until I was exhausted, and somehow I thought that was okay. It was my only example, so surely it must be the correct way to live, right? My growing clientele showed me, as I encouraged them to live differently and prioritize their needs, that I needed to live what I preached. I had to walk the talk. I could not have my clients see me treating myself as an afterthought and be in constant self-repair mode.

My passion for my healing work has continued to grow, and I have gained a unique perspective as I have truly learned how to care for myself and help others find their way to self-care. The path is different for everyone, yet there are tools I use with everyone that I have made the core of my teachings:

- Make space for yourself in your life; not the tasks that need to be completed, but the person you are or want to be.
- Everyone needs community. We are not solitary by design. We need others. Find those that feed your heart and nurture those relationships.
- Reclaim the art of celebrating. This differs from partying, although a party might be perfect on occasion! Honoring the transitions in our lives is essential. Mark the significant events, the signpost moments we look back on as we age.

These things have changed for me in the last ten years and are still evolving. Now my joy is abundant, rooted, and grounded in self-acceptance. I love the quirkiness of who I am and I even adore the sassy—and crassy—parts of me! I have returned to teaching and circle sharing, supporting people to live authentically. To the depths of my being, I know that the last 30 years of my life have the most for me to share, and I am overjoyed to be turning 70!

STAR THOMAS-WYSE

Star Thomas-Wyse has understood healing and energy work her whole life, always being the one people turned to for relief from headaches, shoulder tension, and back aches. Her first professional career was as a manicurist, and she was known for giving the absolute best hand massages. That quickly turned into a lifelong passion and now Star is a massage therapist and energy healer with 50 years of experience and a toolkit that includes certification in many healing modalities. Additional skills she has developed over her career include teaching, coaching, oracle card reading. She also has a deep passion for aromatherapy and practices what she calls AromaAlchemy in her healing work.

She is a co-founder of Bloom Temple, an anointing priestess mystery school, a seminary graduate, licensed minister, and Wiccan high priestess. She has experience creating and leading rituals and life passages including weddings and celebration of life services. She has facilitated classes and gently coached people through important life journeys and transitions.

Star currently lives in the Kansas City metro area and is owned by three very fussy cats! She has lived in California (her first home was on the beach!), the high desert of Santa Fe, New Mexico, and in Oslo, Norway. She has been blessed to travel a sizable portion of the world, meeting people and stretching her capacity to love. Everywhere she has traveled, whether somewhere on the planet or into the depths of her inner landscape, she has emerged with a deeper understanding of the immense beauty life holds and a renewed desire to help people see that beauty within and without. She believes life is an adventure and this year is adding sacred travel experiences to her offerings.

Stepping into 70 years on the planet, she has finally accepted the sassy, crassy crone she is and delights in helping people find their way to true self-care. Ready, set, shine!

Connect with Star at **starthomaswyse.com** and on Facebook at **facebook.com/anointingpriestess.**

Dynamic Life Skills

Dynamic Life Skills is designed to guide you in remembering or discovering easy-to-use tools to bring ease to your Central Nervous System and encourage greater alignment with Mind, Body, and Spirit. In other words, these tools will help you live in the center of the teeter totter, gently keeping balance even if the world is fluctuating wildly around you.

To access: **www.starthomaswyse.com/dynamiclifeskills**

CHAPTER 15

From the Caterpillar to the Butterfly

By Patricia Zachery

I want to start this by sharing an intention I say every morning before I get out of bed and every night before I go to sleep…

Humanity—WE feel and know that OUR highest good is now coming to Us. WE hold OUR miracle intention—that all governments of the world are transformed, benevolent, loving custodians of the people they serve, living in global Peace, Unity, and Universal Abundance—with Love in Our hearts. We see it manifested in Our lives in perfect timing. We give thanks, and so it is.

As a human being, my way of BEing is to live my mission. This is a story about how my beliefs and various jobs have led me to discover my life's mission—to protect my human brothers and sisters, by shining a light on our current government operating system from within the Department of Human Services. I didn't even know I *had* a mission until I was in my last government job at the Veterans Administration, when an inner voice said, "You have two jobs at the VA: one is to assist Veterans where you can, and the other is to transform the VA!"

WTF? Transform the VA? You've got to be kidding.

"Okay, help transform the VA!" the voice said.

That sounds better. Deep exhale. I don't know what I was thinking because it *wasn't* any better, but it felt doable, somehow. I believe the United States Veterans Administration and the government at large, needs to be changed because it's a system that indoctrinates people into slavery by shackling them to programs and services that keep them in survival mode. Since I've received my mission, I have been doing what I can, with what I have, from where I'm at. And what I can do now is begin to shine a light on the government model that we currently have and see where we go from there.

In hindsight, I saw how my beliefs drew me into the Department of Human Services through a *Science of Mind* class I took in 2010, after I had already worked in Corrections and Child Protection. I had just quit my job as a Vocational Counselor at a Job Corps Center, and hadn't yet started at the VA. In this class, we did a meditation and then an exercise in automatic writing to have a conversation with "Life." I had heard about automatic writing, and believed it was possible to show me what might be lurking in my unconscious, so I was willing to give it a try. Imagine my surprise when I finished, and I read the letter written from "Life" to me.

Dear Patti -

Thank you so much for all you've given to those citizens on your planet who keep getting the message they are unloved, and unwanted— rejected and abandoned. You know what that feels like, and you've dedicated your life to helping them see they are so much more and have so much more to give the world. Over the years, you have developed the knowledge, and skills to be more effective in presenting this message and I want to encourage you to continue this path because it's your passion and people are waiting to hear it. Thank you again.

In Love and Light,
"Life"

Wow—this is exactly how I saw myself in my jobs, but I had never heard it reflected back to me before. Nor had I ever made the connection, consciously, that the clients I worked with also felt unloved, unwanted, rejected, and abandoned, by their families and society. I was also beginning to make the connection that I, also, had felt this way in my life. It wasn't just about "those people." It was about ALL of us. From this lens, I could see how I was unconsciously recreating a dynamic with my mother through the clients I worked with, because it was from her that I got the beliefs of feeling unloved, unwanted, rejected, and abandoned. And then I could see how the systems I worked in were also a recapitulation of my father dynamics as well as my larger family dynamics; "*Don't think for yourself, don't tell the truth, don't rock the boat, don't be all that you can be, and we don't say what we mean or mean what we say.*" Holy Smokes! I was recreating both my parents in every job I'd ever had! I knew that people often attracted partners like the parents they liked the least, but I was now seeing that I had done this with both my parents in all my jobs. This realization was mind blowing and it has taken me a few years to process and then a few more years to actually begin changing my patterns of behavior.

I retired from the government in 2016, not because I was ready to stop working, but because I could no longer give my time and attention to the model I had discovered I was working in, which was keeping people in survival mode and not assisting them to move towards a life in which they could thrive. A year after my retirement, I moved to another city to start a new beginning, so I could live my life for me, free from the patterns of dysfunctional parental dynamics. My new motto was, "*I only do what I want to do and what feels good.*" But one day I woke up to the realization that in the first six months of my new beginning, I had applied and interviewed for five jobs that were all government jobs! I was *still* falling back into the old pattern of parental dynamics, but now my vibration was high enough that I didn't get pulled back into the repeated cycle of behavior. Now I am in the last 25 years of my life, and I want to be conscious of the life I'm living because I want to make a difference in the time I have left, so I am committed to consciously waking up—again and again.

In the 40 years that I worked in the government, I was in Corrections, Child Protection, Job Corps, the VA in the homeless program, and then later in a non-profit providing safe spot communities for people to transition off the street. I always thought it was a failed system because it wasn't helping people to move out of their lives of survival and into a happy, healthy life of thriving. Yet, it took me 40 years to realize I had a different definition of success, that meant people would have the skills and opportunities to move out of the system of dependency and become self-sufficient and successful on their own. Why would this not be the case? Ultimately, I could see that success for the government is to keep people desperate and in survival mode so they would continue to feed the programs, because the programs and services need government funding, and the funding is driven by the people needing the programs and services. The Department of Human Services has become a co-dependent partner with the clients they serve, each being dependent on the other for survival.

Here is how I see this co-dependent model coming about in the first place. Back in the days of the Great Depression, people stood in bread lines for the very first time in this country. I believe there were good-hearted people in the government who said, "OMG—we have to do something to help these people," and they put together programs and services to help those in need. They saw that they would need funding to implement these programs and services, so they went to the funding sources to present their idea and ask for funding and were told, "Funding is available, but it will be assessed based on need." Thus began the documentation of clients needing services and programs and the funding was driven by the numbers of people in need.

Back when this model was being built, the focus was only on helping the people who were in immediate need so there was no attention given to creating an exit plan once their immediate needs were met. **This model has never changed.** That's a 1930's model that the Department of Human Services is operating under today—and it's still being driven by numbers. The higher the number, the more funding.

It should have been a red flag when we hit generational welfare and poverty that this system wasn't working successfully—but that would have been looking through the lens of success being measured by happiness and self-sufficiency, not success being measured by on-going desperation and dependency. If we're looking through the lens of success as dependency, which keeps people in survival mode with their children being born into it, then according to the government, this model is a success. It took me a very long time to see this because I didn't want to believe this is what our government agencies were doing.

As I began to see more clearly, I was drawn back to my studies in my master's program in Transpersonal Counseling Psychology at The Naropa Institute, where we studied the Developmental Stages of Growth. For the first time, I could see how these stages were showing up in the Department of Human Services. The Developmental Stages of Growth, that I'm referring to, as described by Erik Erickson, show how each stage has a spectrum of development from low to high. I have included which departments of DHS are in each stage and have highlighted the level of development that is likely because of the trauma and abuse that is perpetrated not only in the families they come from but the departments within the system itself.

Stage 1: **Mistrust vs Trust– Infancy**—Social Services/Child Protection/Foster Care/Homeless

Stage 2: **Shame and Doubt vs Autonomy**—Early Childhood—Social Services/Child Protection/Foster Care/Homeless

Stage 3: **Guilt vs Initiative**—Pre-School—Social Services/Child Protection/Foster Care/Homeless

Stage 4: **Inferiority vs Industry**—School Age—Social Services/Child Protection/Foster Care/Homeless

Stage 5: **Role Confusion vs Identity**—Adolescents—Social Services/Child Protection/ Foster Care/Job Corps/Juvenile Detention/Homeless

The last three stages are affected by the first five stages:

Stage 6: **Isolation vs Intimacy**—Young Adult—Social Services/Job Corps/Jail-Prison/Homeless

Stage 7: **Stagnation vs Generativity**—Middle Adult—Social Services/Jail-Prison/Homeless

Stage 8: **Despair vs Integrity**—Adulthood/Maturity—Social Services/Jail-Prison/Homeless

These stages are in full operation in the Department of Human Services and the people who receive their services fall to the lower end of the growth scale. How is it that no one can see how unsuccessful these agencies are as they influence people to develop **mistrust, shame and doubt, guilt, inferiority, role confusion, isolation, stagnation, and despair**? Where, within this system, are people being taught trust, autonomy, initiative, industry, identity, intimacy, generativity, and integrity? Where are they supposed to learn these qualities if they are, indeed, to become contributing members of society?

Not only have I worked in the agencies that reflect these stages of growth, but they also reflect my own developmental stages of growth. When working in Corrections, I was like an adolescent rebelling against my father, and after a while I saw that the system didn't support the people it served to change for the better. In fact, what I saw was people being treated the way they were used to being treated, which was a guarantee they would return—and that was job security.

When working in Child Protection, I got in touch with my own pain and heartache of being emotionally neglected and abandoned, and what I saw was these children had no power to change their lives or circumstances and the system wasn't looking out for them but working to get the family back together. This was the most traumatizing job I've ever had because as a child protection social worker, I ended up damaging kids because the real goal was to bring the family back together, no matter how that affected the child. Or the child was taken away from an abusive family only to be placed in Foster Care, in many cases, in an even more abusive situation than the family they came from. And then there's the trauma to the child from being placed in numerous homes during their time in Foster Care. When I say it was the most traumatizing job I've ever had, I mean that twenty-five plus years later when I talk about it, I still cry. If I was affected like that after only one year in that system, imagine a child being in it for 18 years, and then dumped on the street because they've aged out of the system. If you want a real example of how this system works, look up the documentary, *The Trial of Gabriel Fernandez* on Netflix. This is a heartbreaking example which I believe is the norm more than the exception.

Then I went on to Job Corps, where I got in touch with my disconnected youth, especially the time when my parents left me at 17 and moved to Hawaii. I really thought that Job Corps was the place change could happen because this was a residential program. The kids, aged 16-24, were away from their families and yet were at an age when the development of abstract thought could begin to help them recognize patterns of behavior. I believed this was where I could really make a difference, unlike Child Protection where the children had no power and Corrections where they also had no power and had already lived a long life of unhealthy patterns of behavior. But I was naive.

By the time I got to the VA, I was able to pull a lot of what I had learned about myself together and could see how my experiences had influenced who I was becoming, and see how I was called to the jobs that would show me my mission, and give me the big picture perspective on how these departments operate and why it's imperative that we create a new model.

Imperative, that is, if people want to start getting different results than we've been getting so far. It's time to start healing hearts and stop shattering them. If one person is broken, we are ALL broken.

One way to look at this from a different perspective is to ask the question, "How well would a 1930's model car work on our highways and freeways today?" It wouldn't work well at all and yet, we are still using a 1930's model operating system which has been focused on pulling people into it for 93 years but has done little to support those people or help them move out of the system when they try to get out. Most of the time when a person in the Social Services System gets a job with the intention of getting ahead, and they make a tad over a certain amount, the crucial services they are already dependent on will be cut, such as food stamps and health care. There is no incentive or support to get out of the system and yet the system is overflowing its capacity with more people than they can serve. And so, nothing changes.

A question that comes to my mind is, "Who is supposed to be evaluating the different agencies in our government system to make sure they are working for the best interest of the clients?" Perhaps it's time for these departmental evaluations to happen through a non-federal agency that has no investment in the outcome. I know they can still be bribed, which seems to be happening in so many other areas of our government—like the relationship between corporations and lawmakers today—but this might be a start.

I remember when I was at Job Corps, we had people come to evaluate the Center and we knew six months in advance of their arrival, which gave plenty of time to get prepared by sprucing the place up with a new coat of paint and grooming the students to give the right answers to questions likely to be asked. When I was interviewed, as a Vocational Counselor, I would always say, "If you really wanted to find out how this Center runs, you would come unannounced, or you would send a young member of your interviewing committee to come as an undercover student!" My comments were always ignored. Perhaps it wasn't as much about evaluating each Center to assist it to be better, as it was about being on a road trip to different Centers, staying in hotels, and being paid for the vacation.

I don't know what it's going to take to change this system. Whatever I say or however I say it, it's not being heard because this model is programmed to run this way. When I suggested doing something differently, which might be more efficient, the response I got every time was, "Well, this is the way we've always done it."

I have made the suggestion of converting one of Oregon's four Job Corps Centers into a Vocational Training Center for Veterans to get job training and Mental Health treatment for addictions or PTSD, to assist them back into the civilian work force after leaving the military, as well as assist homeless Veterans to get off the street, to have housing, treatment services and vocational training needed to get them back on their feet. I have gotten little to no response.

Maybe Buckminster Fuller was right when he said, "You never change things by fighting the existing reality. To change something, build a new model that makes the existing model obsolete."

How and where do we begin building a new model that will make this model obsolete? How do we move into the model where all governments of the world are transformed, benevolent, loving custodians of the people they serve, living in global Peace, Unity, and Universal abundance?

Human + Divinity = Humanity

How do we create a government that supports cooperation, collaboration, and partnership, to find WIN/WIN/WIN solutions for any situation? Now that would be an exciting world to live in!

Imagine how much fun it would be to be to participate in conversations that are asking questions like these:

1. What would it take to get a WIN/WIN/WIN outcome in this situation?
2. Who do we need to become to get this result?
3. What kind of model do we need to co-create for our government and other businesses to get WIN/WIN/WIN outcomes?

You can't know what you don't know. But once you know, you can't NOT know.

Now you know.

What part will you play in this transformation to co-create a new government model, a new business model, or a new non-profit model that is co-creating WIN/WIN/WIN outcomes? How can you begin to build your own compassion muscle for yourself, and for other people?

I say, open your heart and be willing to face what's happening right under your nose—because that will begin the healing for humanity. And *please*, watch *The Trial of Gabriel Fernandez* on Netflix, to see firsthand how this system currently operates.

PATRICIA CATHERINE ZACHERY

Patricia has a master's degree in Transpersonal Counseling Psychology, obtained from the Naropa Institute in Boulder, CO. She has worked as a government employee for 40 years in Corrections, as a Social Worker in Child Protection, as a Vocational Counselor in Job Corps, as a Case Worker at the Veteran's Administration, and as a Support Worker in a non-profit providing safe spot communities for the homeless to get off the street—all while attending retreats, trainings, and workshops to receive a Hypnotherapy Certification, a Breath Work Certification, a Massage Certification, a Reiki Master Certification and a Peer Support Certification. Having spent much of her life focused on the survival aspects of our broken government system, she's now ready to step into the world of thriving and focus her attention on how to co-create a new model that is working in collaboration, cooperation, and partnership for WIN/WIN/WIN outcomes, as she is planning to move into a tiny home co-op community that is currently under construction.

When she's not thinking about how to co-create this new model, she can be found writing in her journal while in the hot tub, where she has been writing her memoirs over the last four years called *The Awakening of a Soul—Memoirs from the Hot Tub*.

You can contact Patricia at **pczachery@aol.com**

FREE GIFT

My gift to you is sharing the people who have been TURNING POINTS in my life.

Alicia Power: Soul Mentoring, where I listened to an mp3 called, "I AM GOD" over and over just to normalize the truth of the statement that I AM GOD. **soulmentoring.com**

Dr. Sue Morter: The author of *The Energy Codes*, where I embodied the truth that I am living my life as my Soulful Self. **drsuemorter.com**

Lee Harris: Lee's monthly energy updates and his channels of the Z's have helped me recognize the powers within me and have helped me navigate through the changes we are seeing in the world around us. **leeharrisenergy.com**

Sonia Choquette: As I've stepped into living in this human body as my Soulful Self, Sonia's teachings have been like a treasure map, showing me the way to my higher self and connecting me with Beings and Guides just waiting for me to invite them into my journey. **soniachoquette.net**

My wish is that any one of these people may be Turning Point for your life to become all it's meant to be.

Volume 1 of the *Turning Point* anthology series is available at www.amazon.com/dp/B0BMZ369XX

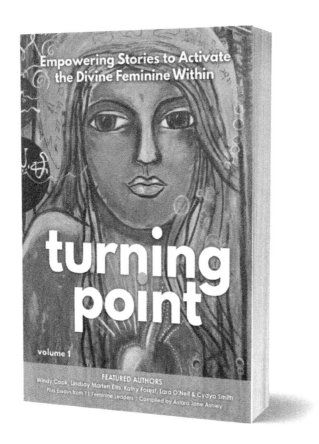

Printed in Great Britain
by Amazon

25216134R00118